WHY READ PASCAL TODAY?

Blaise Pascal (1623–1662) was one of the greatest geniuses of the modern era. He made important contributions to mathematics, the theory of probability, and several scientific fields, and invented the first mathematical calculator. He was also a deeply religious thinker who grappled with issues concerning the existence of God, the possibility of human salvation, and the problems of human life. His famous wager on the existence of God is often discussed in philosophy, but there is much else of interest and relevance in his thought. This book provides an accessible yet detailed account of Pascal's philosophy and how it applies to important issues facing all of us today, as well as novel interpretations of Pascal's ideas. It will stimulate and challenge anyone who is interested in the role of the heart in rationality, deep disagreement, human nature, our individual and collective purpose, and other underexplored thoughts of one of history's greatest geniuses.

YUVAL AVNUR is the author of *The Skeptic and the Veridicalist* (Cambridge, 2023) and numerous essays on epistemology and religion, and co-editor (with Roger Ariew) of *A Companion to Pascal* (Wiley Blackwell, 2025).

WHY READ THEM TODAY?

The books in this series offer new interpretations of thinkers who in different ways reward contemporary re-examination, showing how their thought is particularly relevant to us today.

Books in This Series

STEVEN NADLER, *Why Read Maimonides Today?*

SANDRINE BERGÈS, *Why Read Wollstonecraft Today?*

YUVAL AVNUR, *Why Read Pascal Today?*

WHY READ PASCAL TODAY?

YUVAL AVNUR
Scripps College, California

CAMBRIDGE UNIVERSITY PRESS

Shaftesbury Road, Cambridge CB2 8EA, United Kingdom

One Liberty Plaza, 20th Floor, New York, NY 10006, USA

477 Williamstown Road, Port Melbourne, VIC 3207, Australia

314–321, 3rd Floor, Plot 3, Splendor Forum, Jasola District Centre, New Delhi – 110025, India

103 Penang Road, #05–06/07, Visioncrest Commercial, Singapore 238467

Cambridge University Press is part of Cambridge University Press & Assessment, a department of the University of Cambridge.

We share the University's mission to contribute to society through the pursuit of education, learning and research at the highest international levels of excellence.

www.cambridge.org
Information on this title: www.cambridge.org/9781009321488

DOI: 10.1017/9781009321495

© Cambridge University Press & Assessment 2026

This publication is in copyright. Subject to statutory exception and to the provisions of relevant collective licensing agreements, no reproduction of any part may take place without the written permission of Cambridge University Press & Assessment.

When citing this work, please include a reference to the DOI 10.1017/9781009321495

First published 2026

A catalogue record for this publication is available from the British Library

A Cataloging-in-Publication data record for this book is available from the Library of Congress

ISBN 978-1-009-32148-8 Hardback
ISBN 978-1-009-32144-0 Paperback

Cambridge University Press & Assessment has no responsibility for the persistence or accuracy of URLs for external or third-party internet websites referred to in this publication and does not guarantee that any content on such websites is, or will remain, accurate or appropriate.

For EU product safety concerns, contact us at Calle de José Abascal, 56, 1°, 28003 Madrid, Spain, or email eugpsr@cambridge.org

Man is only a reed, the weakest thing in nature, but he is a thinking reed. The whole universe does not need to take up arms to crush him; a vapor, a drop of water, is enough to kill him. But if the universe were to crush him, man would still be nobler than what killed him, because he knows he is dying and the advantage the universe has over him. The universe knows nothing of this.

All our dignity consists, then, in thought. It is from this that we must raise ourselves, and not from space and duration, which we could not fill. Let us labor, then, to think well. This is the principle of morality. (Blaise Pascal, *Pensées* S231-2/L200)

Contents

Acknowledgments — page ix

- Introduction — 1
  - 0.1 Renown and Neglect — 4
  - 0.2 Is This History? — 8
  - 0.3 An Overview — 10

1. The Limits of Reason and Experience — 13
   - 1.1 Geometry, Space, and Spatial Infinities — 15
   - 1.2 Dreams and the "External World" — 22
   - 1.3 Lost between Two Infinities — 28
   - 1.4 Theological and Metaphysical Proofs — 38

2. The Heart — 46
   - 2.1 Belief and the Heart — 47
   - 2.2 Geometry and the External World as Matters of the Heart — 52
   - 2.3 Divine Hiddenness in the Light of the Heart — 55
   - 2.4 The Fall: A Tale of Two Hearts — 60
   - 2.5 The Heart's Own Reasons — 65

3. The Ambiguous World — 72
   - 3.1 The Metaphysical Significance of Ambiguity — 73
   - 3.2 Disagreement (of Hearts and Minds), Rationality, and Non-relativism — 78
   - 3.3 Echo Chambers and Conspiracy Theories: A Pascalian Perspective — 85

4. Desires and Distractions — 91
   - 4.1 Our Defective Natures: Don't Follow Your Heart! — 94
   - 4.2 Unhappiness Leads to Distraction — 99
   - 4.3 Another Confirmation of the Fall — 103

5	**Wager with All Your Heart**	106
	5.1 Motivating a Change of Heart	109
	5.2 Infinity, Nothingness (or "The Wager")	112
	5.3 The Benefits of Seeking	119
	5.4 The Objections and Two Appeals to Self-Deception	122
6	**A Secular Pascalian Vision**	132
	6.1 Constraints on a Good Theory	134
	6.2 The Good Prevails: James' Belief	135
	6.3 Secular Wagers	137

Suggested Further Reading — 142
Index — 144

Acknowledgments

I first decided to study Pascal more closely when I was already a professor. In an attempt to do a better job answering questions about the "the wager" in my introductory classes, I started reading the rest of the *Pensées*. I therefore owe thanks to my students, whose questions inspired me to dig deeper. Much of Pascal's philosophy revolves around the heart, so I must also thank the people closest to it: My wife and children. Finally, I owe thanks to the many philosophers who have discussed Pascal with me and, in some cases, given comments directly on this manuscript. These brilliant friends of mine include Roger Ariew, John Martin Fischer, Paul Hurley, Daniel Klugman, Mara van der Lugt, Kevin McCain, Billy Ross, John Schellenberg, Dion Scott-Kakures, Rivka Weinberg, Howard Wettstein, and Bryan Williams.

Introduction

"Pascal is one of those writers who will be and who must be studied afresh by men in every generation. It is not he who changes, but we who change. It is not our knowledge of him that increases, but our world that alters and our attitudes towards it."[1]

This is how T. S. Eliot introduced Pascal's work a few generations ago, anticipating the task of this book: why, and how, should we read Pascal today? One of Pascal's key ideas is that what is in your heart can change the way the world appears, so Eliot's remark is not only convenient for this introduction but also philosophically astute. However, though there is something for almost everyone in Pascal, this can be difficult to discern. For the contemporary reader, Pascal's texts often appear disjointed and distracted by obscure theological disputes. But they contain intense embers that seem to have been lying in wait to catch our dry and brittle contemporary hearts. His beautiful words have delighted, inspired, and sometimes horrified readers throughout the centuries. Today, if you look not only closely but also broadly enough, they enlighten.

Blaise Pascal (1623–62) was one of the most important and brilliant thinkers of the early modern period. But of all the famous early modern philosophers, he is probably the least read and understood today. He is also one of the greatest stylists (in French) of them all. The *Pensées*, his best-known work, is fun to read: full of explosive and surprising ideas in short, sometimes tweet-sized notes. He presents a picture of humankind and its place in nature that is at once classic (largely based on

---

[1] Eliot, Thomas Stearns (1964). The *Pensées* of Pascal. In *Selected Essays, (T.S. Eliot, ed.)*. New York: Harcourt, Brace, and World; 355.

Augustinian theology), modern (containing similarities with and reactions against his contemporary Descartes), and well ahead of its time not only in its use of probability and confirmation but also in its proto-existentialist tendencies and surprisingly accurate descriptions of the contemporary human condition. His ideas can be applied to many pressing, current problems in and beyond academic philosophy, including our place in nature (and our corruption of it), the ways in which our beliefs can be manipulated, and what control we have or lack over our lives.

It is relatively easy to sum up Pascal's overall philosophy: without God, humanity and every individual is irredeemably corrupted, hopelessly lost, and miserable. The only way out of this sad state – and you may be too corrupted to even know that you are miserable and in need of saving – is by turning your heart toward God and by His grace, He can save you. If we leave it at that level of detail, there is nothing unique here; it is a standard and familiar Christian theology. But his philosophy is worth working through for several reasons. The way in which we come to know (or in many cases remain ignorant) of our condition and how to cure it is entirely nonstandard, even alien to the philosophy of today. We can learn a lot from this epistemology. The place of reason and understanding in Pascal is complicated but surprisingly minor, while the heart – an affective faculty that loves, fears, wills, is attracted, and is repulsed, which consequently determines the range of things one can believe and even see – plays the foundational and central role in our cognitive and practical lives. He was neither empiricist nor rationalist, long before Kant made that cool. His religious philosophy is, for the standard approach of today, daringly anti-epistemological (especially for an eminent mathematician and scientist) and anti-metaphysical, with proofs and evidence taking a back seat. His insights into the tortured human condition are as eerily relevant today as ever, so we have much to gain by reflecting on ourselves in their light.

It may seem to today's secular reader that there is nothing of philosophical interest in Pascal's work because it all unfolds within an explicitly religious context. But this is true only on the most superficial and selective skimming of the text. It pays to keep in mind that Descartes, Pascal's esteemed contemporary, had an epistemological picture that also featured God at the center, and yet philosophers have managed to make much use of his ideas in a secular context. The same, I will suggest, applies to Pascal: there is a lot to gain from his thought even outside of a religious context, even setting aside the somewhat obscure theological debates he was engaged in. In fact, his epistemological (or anti-epistemological) insights in the religious domain can be applied analogously, and with much to gain, to our situation as would-be knowers today. For example, the way in which a nonbeliever is lost and insulated from the only evidence that can help, in Pascal, resembles in promising ways the conspiracy theorist's, the political extremist's, the arrogantly confident ignoramus', and even the seeker of meaning's situation today – not that these are all on a par. From a Pascalian perspective, their mistake is not that they have forgotten to recheck the evidence or failed to do more research. Rather, it is that they aren't looking at things in the right way, and that is because their hearts are in the wrong place.

This is not to say that his religious ideas as such are irrelevant today. Arguably his apologetics will appeal better to today's nonbelievers than the typical attempt at evangelism, and this will naturally interest today's believers as well. Conversations and debates about religion (and Christianity especially) tend to revolve around arguments for God's existence, including appeals to apparent design – how could all of this marvelous complexity have come about randomly? – and arguments against God's existence, including the problem of evil – how could catastrophic evil have come about divinely? Pascal offers a perspective from which these disputes fail to engage their subject matter, in two ways: they misunderstand the religion and "God" they're directed at, and they misunderstand the nature of belief and the role of arguments and reason in its formation. He operates on the more direct, visceral level on which the world seems ambiguous: containing mysterious, unfathomable beauty and immeasurable, unspeakable horrors. What should we make of this ambiguity? Why are we capable of seeing and judging the world in these ways? Pascal today promises to reset a stale and predictable dialectic about a matter as important as any, and as ever, to human life.

This advertisement for Pascal's promise might surprise you, even though you have very likely heard of him before. This is because, though everyone knows his name, almost no one in the Anglosphere has read him thoroughly or carefully, and many have never read him at all. He is both famous and underread. These facts about the state of Pascal literacy deserve at least a brief explanation before we get to know him and his texts a little better.

0.1 Renown and Neglect

There is a variety of ways to have heard of Pascal. He invented the calculator, found early empirical evidence for the existence of a vacuum, was a giant of mathematics responsible for the foundation of modern probability theory, and even thought up arguably the first scheme for public transit (the "five penny coaches"). But his brilliance shined in other ways, too. As already mentioned, he is regarded as one of the greatest stylists in the French language, a brilliant polemicist, and an important religious thinker. In a typical introductory course in philosophy, chances are good that you will encounter an argument named after him, "Pascal's wager." Other things are named after him today too, corresponding to his seminal contributions to each field: a popular programming language, a triangular mathematical array, a standard unit of pressure. All of this and he never lived to see his fortieth birthday! As you can see, despite his short life often burdened by serious illness, Pascal thought big. His ideas are rigorous, deep, and wide in scope. As Pope Francis recently put it in an apostolic letter, on the occasion of Pascal's quadricentennial in 2023, Pascal was "a man marked by a fundamental attitude of awe and openness to all reality."

Despite being so renowned, Pascal is severely underread. His contribution to philosophy is often reduced with the so-called wager, an argument that, as we will see in Chapter 5, is usually taken out of both historical context and the context of Pascal's own texts, and consequently misunderstood. It is a matter of great frustration, for those few who have dived deep into Pascal's world, that his contribution is often reduced by philosophers to this argument apparently for the conclusion that it is worthwhile, in your own interest, to try to believe in God. It turns out this wasn't exactly his argument, and most discussions of this "wager" miss his point.

This misunderstanding is not entirely readers' fault. The note that is usually referred to as the source of "the wager" is a fragment entitled

0.1 Renown and Neglect

"*infini rien*" from a bundle of notes found on his desk after his death. Several bundles of these notes were found in this way. They were written, sometimes jotted haphazardly, for a planned Christian apology. The aim was to convince the "libertines" or nonbelievers of his day to find God in the Catholic tradition. He died before he wrote it, so all we have are the preparatory notes.[2] For generations since, these collected notes have been edited and ordered in different ways by different scholars, and the result is Pascal's *Pensées*, or "thoughts," the main source we have for his philosophy. But these notes appear fragmented and the connections between them unclear at first. So, it is understandable if a reader takes something out of context. Out of many hundreds of notes, *infini rien*, or what came to be known as "the wager," is one – we will see later in this book why he titled it *infini rien* instead of *pari* (which is the word for "wager"). Beyond correcting the record on "the wager," much of the present work aims to show that Pascal's *Pensées* offers so much more: it is a treasure trove of insight into belief, our nature as divergent believers, our place in whatever the universe is, the human condition in general, the place of religion in life, the source of our desires and the problems they give rise to, and the basic problem we face in relating to reality.

Not only does the unusual format of the *Pensées* go some way toward explaining the widespread misunderstanding of "the wager," it might also account for why so many never read beyond it and miss the bigger picture. Depending on the edition you read, the passages often skip around to different topics and sometimes even appear inconsistent with each other. This can create an impression that there is no larger picture and no "system" to Pascal's thought. But this is a false impression, even if the format makes his system harder to discover. This book is intended to help with the process of deciphering the bigger picture in the *Pensées*, by bringing some of these apparently disparate elements together into one coherent and relatable picture, sometimes with the help of other works of Pascal.

---

[2] Though there is also an account of his presentation to his colleagues at the Port Royal detailing his plan for this work, by his nephew. This is in the preface to the early Port Royal edition of *The Pensées*. It can be found in the *Oevres Complétes* edited by Guern Michel Le (1998–2000). *Bibliothéque de la Pléiade*. Paris: Gallimard, volume II 902–906.

One might speculate that the neglect of Pascal is entirely explained by the fact that the *Pensées* is a collection of notes. But that is not plausible. After all, so is much of Wittgenstein's work, and he is certainly not neglected. What else keeps people from reading Pascal today?

Another reason for neglect might be his reputation. He is regarded as a dark, stern, finger-wagging figure. There is a tradition of reading Pascal as both depressing and fanatical. Adam Smith regarded Pascal as a "whining and melancholy moralist" and Smith's friend David Hume once quipped that Pascal was unduly influenced by "the most ridiculous superstitions." (In fact, as we will see, Hume's philosophy was remarkably similar to, and probably borrowed from, Pascal's.) Likewise Voltaire, who appreciated Pascal as a stylist, called him a "sublime misanthrope," whose wager for God was "indecent and childish."

It is undeniable that Pascal did some moralizing. An early biographer of Pascal, his own sister, describes a severe figure whose view of human nature was uncompromising, and whose moral sense most of us would find grotesque: he once chastised her for letting her children show her too much affection. It is hard for us to relate to this today, but in Pascal's view it would have been better for the children to cultivate a love of divinity instead of an attachment to earthly things, since "we must love only God and hate only ourselves" (S405/L373).[3]

If that seems offensive, don't worry but get used to telling yourself not to worry. This is part of Pascal, but it is not the *whole* story, and it is not *all* of you that he suggests you hate. As for accusations of misanthropy and whining, they are as unjust as they have been influential. While it is true that Pascal dwelled on the apparent absence of divinity in the world for some of us, he also held that you could see God everywhere if only your heart were in the right place. The problem is that most of us in the modern world have our hearts in the wrong place. His efforts to draw our attention to this may have resulted in some harsh descriptions of our condition, but as we will see, those descriptions were aimed at bringing about an awareness of our shortcomings so that we realize our potential greatness. And they ring truer today perhaps than ever.

---

[3] Throughout this book, I will be using Roger Ariew's translation when quoting the *Pensées*, from Pascal, Blaise (2004). *Pensées*. Hackett: Indianapolis. Like Ariew, I cite each quoted fragment using the Sellier edition's numbering first, followed by the Lafuma edition's numbering.

0.1 Renown and Neglect

As already mentioned, one of Pascal's insights is that what you see in the world depends on what is in your heart when you investigate. The same applies to his own work and what attitude we bring when we read it. It is true that Pascal thought humanity was corrupted to the core (as I explain in Chapter 4), but he also wrote that we are capable of greatness:

> Man's greatness is so obvious that it can be derived even from his wretchedness. (S249/L117)

How do we react to this? Is it optimistic? Insulting? Depressing? Inspiring? Perhaps Pascal would have wanted all these reactions. But I suggest that before deciding how to react, we should put such statements in their place within a larger Pascalian worldview. We have it in our hearts to become great, but as he will remind us, we need help. In fact, I will suggest that one of his key philosophical moves is to argue that, left only to our own devices and faculties, we know nothing (Chapter 1) and are nothing (Chapter 4); by reaching out beyond ourselves, we can know a lot (including our limits, see Chapter 3) and have a chance at greatness (Chapter 5). So he wasn't so much a misanthrope, but rather thought that a human *in isolation* is hopeless and wretched. Pascal offers a worldview that gives love and connection to something beyond oneself a central place, since it is love that connects us with all we need in order to be great (Chapter 2). For Pascal, the solution to our problems is religious. The thing beyond yourself that you must love is God. But, along the way and in the final chapter of this book, I will suggest ways in which the core of the solution need not be specifically religious. So if it is Pascal's darkness and pessimism that has prevented you from delving into his thought, I hope this book shows that this is not a good reason, because it is not all doom and gloom (though there is some of that, too).

Why else might one resist reading Pascal? Many of his texts deal with seemingly obscure theological disputes, which hold little interest to most of today's contemporary philosophers. This is fair enough. But to see through this and to get to some real and fundamental philosophical insights, only a minimal understanding of the theological context is required, and I will provide it as needed in what follows. As we will see, the main background that is required to understand Pascal's philosophy is a classic Augustinian theology.

0.2 Is This History?

If this book aimed to argue thoroughly that Pascal meant this rather than that, it would require a substantial understanding of the theological and philosophical debates of Pascal's day. But exegesis is not our primary aim.[4] Rather, we will extract some central ideas within his writings in order to see how they might fit together and what is so philosophically fascinating and relevant about them. I will argue that there are ideas within Pascal that matter philosophically *today*, so that it is worth reading him. Sometimes this will involve developing his ideas a bit further, beyond the text itself, and sometimes this will go in a direction that Pascal never intended and probably would not have agreed with. But it will be clear when that happens, and always for the purpose of arguing, not that some claim or idea is what Pascal meant, and not that we should endorse or accept it, but that it presents a reason to read Pascal carefully and engage with his ideas.

Accordingly, the aim is not to describe intellectual history. To be sure, that history is both interesting and important for understanding Pascal. Pascal was massively influenced not only by Augustine but also by Jansen's interpretation of Augustine, Montaigne's interpretation of skepticism, by his contemporary, Descartes, the many Cartesians in his circle, and many others. But as Pascal wrote:

> Let no one say I have said nothing new: the arrangement of the material is new. When we play handball, we both play with the same ball, but one of us places it better. I would just as soon be told I have used old words. As if the same thoughts did not form a different discourse by being arranged differently, just as the same words form different thoughts by their being arranged differently! (S575/L696)

---

[4] For this I recommend Michael Moriarty's excellent and already indispensable *Pascal: Reasoning and Belief*, OUP (Clarendon, 2020), which also aims to assess Pascal in light of contemporary developments. For shorter treatments of more focused topics in the study of Pascal's philosophy, see *A Companion to Pascal*, Roger Ariew & Yuval Avnur, eds., Wiley (*Hoboken, New Jersey*, 2025). For an alternative approach to the aims of the present book, see Griffiths, Paul (2021). *Why Read Pascal?* The Catholic University of America Press (DC).

0.2 Is This History?

In defense of the somewhat (I would say rather conservative) revisionary aspect of this book, note that Pascal apparently seemed not to have a problem with the way I propose to use his text:

> Some authors, speaking of their works, say: "My book, my commentary, my story, etc. ... They would do better to say: "Our book, our commentary, our history, etc.," seeing that there is usually more of others in these than of their own.[5]

Finally, a brief prefatory note about the religious nature of much of Pascal's thought as we will explore it. The reader, I assume, is either a contemporary version of Pascal's audience in the *Pensées* (a nonbeliever), or a believer of today that is interested in that perspective. Even if you are a Christian, chances are that you are not the kind of Christian that Pascal wants you to be, and so it is still helpful to regard you as a nonbeliever. In any case I will address Pascal's arguments to the nonbeliever, and assume that contemporary Christians are still interested, because it is important for them to understand how to engage with a nonbeliever, and Pascal has important ideas about this.

To be clear about the target audience of this book, it includes anyone, religious or not, who is philosophically interested, even those who profess a condescending indifference to the religious matters that occupied Pascal. The latter's notion is that we have already figured out pretty much everything, certainly with respect to divinity: there is none, so religious philosophy is all ridiculous and trifling. Pascal addressed this attitude directly: stop pretending you're indifferent! You may have made up your mind (and hopefully Pascal will reopen the matter for you), but don't confuse your misplaced confidence with indifference. It matters what created nature and humankind, whether there is a purpose to human life, and whether this life is all there is for us (S681-2, L427-28). It matters whether you've made a mistake about this.

---

[5] This is one of a few fragments attributed to Pascal but not included in the more definitive editions such as Sellier's. It is unclear whether Pascal wrote it, but it appears in the Lafuma edition as 1,000 and the Brunschvicg edition as 43, so some writers take it for granted that it is Pascal. See fn. 3 in Roger Ariew's *Pierre Duhem's Pascalian Philosophy of Science* in Ariew & Avnur *ibid.*, which is also the source of the translation I use.

0.3 An Overview

Chapters 1–3 are about Pascal's epistemology. "Epistemology" is not exactly the right term, though, because his view was not just about knowledge (*êpisteme*), and not just about rational belief. He was deeply and, in the *Pensées*, primarily concerned with faith. If we can include faith among the topics of epistemology (as some do in what is today called "religious epistemology"), we can credit Pascal's epistemology with some surprising and important elements.

In Chapter 1, we will see that Pascal held that one's own cognitive resources, especially reason and experience operating on their own, are insufficient in various ways. In order to get things right and achieve certainty or knowledge, we need a sort of faith that can only arise with the help of something external to the individual. As is so often the case in Pascal, this is an idea we find also in Augustine:

> [E]rrors and false opinions contaminate life if the reasoning mind is itself flawed ... the soul needs to be enlightened by light from outside itself, so that it can participate in truth, because it is not itself the nature of truth. You will light my lamp, O Lord. (IV. xv (25))[6]

Pascal shows the need for an external source of illumination by adopting, repurposing, and augmenting some skeptical arguments familiar from Montaigne and Descartes. The incapacity of reason and experience on their own to produce knowledge applies not only to abstract first principles but also to sensory appearances and, most importantly for Pascal, the significance (or "measure") of human life and religious faith. Left to our own reasoning and sensory faculties, we are in the dark.

Pascal's epistemology gives a central, foundational role to something outside of reason and experience: "the heart." The heart is the missing ingredient whose necessity skepticism demonstrates. For this reason, we can think of Pascal's epistemology as *cordate* (or "heart-shaped"). The heart makes the difference between a lost soul grasping hopelessly in the dark and a fully enlightened agent who is engaged appropriately with

---

[6] Augustine, Saint (2008). *Confessions: A New Translation by Henry Chadwick*. Oxford World Classics, Oxford: Oxford University Press. For discussion see Pasnau, Robert (2024). Divine Illumination. In Edward N. Zalta & Uri Nodelman (eds.), *The Stanford Encyclopedia of Philosophy* (Summer ed.), forthcoming https://plato.stanford.edu/archives/sum2024/entries/illumination/.

reality. The heart, though it is internal to a person, reaches for and, in a sense, contains something wholly distinct from the individual, something inscrutable to reason, and it can be affected by something external to or distinct from the individual – this is what happens when God affects your heart. Again, Pascal offers a modern development of an Augustinian (and to some extent biblical) idea. Pascal is neither an empiricist nor a rationalist, because at the foundation is an *affective* state or relation, not a rational insight or experience. In the end, the foundation of all our knowledge, and the center of Pascal's epistemology, is the heart, an affective faculty that wills and loves. This is the topic of Chapter 2.

Key to Pascal's philosophy is that the world is ambiguous. Two people looking at the same world might reasonably draw two entirely different and sometimes opposed conclusions. This is because their hearts differ. We will see that, in today's terms, this does not imply relativism nor what some today call "permissivism." It is instead a view about the nature of how things appear, how we process the way things appear into beliefs about the world, and the fundamental ambiguity of the world itself – all part of Pascal's general theological outlook, "the Fall," which can also shed light on some contemporary concerns. The ambiguity of the world, and the role of the heart in it, confirms some worldviews and rules out others. It also has application to today's polarized society. This is the topic of Chapter 3.

Philosophy concerns not just what to believe but also how to live. Chapters 1–3 focused on belief and how it is tangled up with the state of one's heart. But the heart also, and even primarily, is the seat of the will and the source of our decisions. So the determinant of what we believe also helps to determine how we live, and the choices we might make to change how we live. As in the case of belief, we also find both dark and inspiring ideas about the human condition in Pascal. On the one hand, we are "a paradox," and our default state as post-Fall beings is "concupiscence," a heart that loves only the self, and grasps at creation for its own purposes. This makes us miserable and corrupt. On the other hand, we see that we *could* be great, that we could love that which is beyond and is the source of the world around us. In Chapter 4, we will see how the human heart is corrupted and desires all the wrong things. But by thinking well, we can see this and our potential to change for the better.

In Chapter 5, we will consider why, having glimpsed one's corruption and the possibility of rising above this misery, one might want to seek a particular kind of change: to seek God in one's heart and belief. This is the most famous part of the *Pensées*, the so-called wager. We will see that, despite the strategic and self-interested nature of these considerations, the course of action Pascal's argument recommends is not a sort of self-deception. The wager is a decision to put yourself in a position where a change of heart is possible, so that you see things differently, and where you have *infinitely* much to gain and *nothing* to lose (hence the title of the fragment, *infini rien*). The key to avoiding common misunderstandings of the wager is that this is about inviting a change of heart, rather than tricking yourself to believe something, and this invitation potentially benefits you even if your heart never changes.

Finally, in Chapter 6, we will consider what a secularized version of a Pascalian view, wager and all, might look like.

CHAPTER I

The Limits of Reason and Experience

> Man is but a subject full of natural error that cannot be eradicated without grace. [Nothing] shows him the truth. Everything deceives him.
>
> (S78/L45)

If Pascal's primary destination was the Christian religion, the gate was a particular kind of skepticism. (In this respect, he resembles Descartes in the *Meditations*.) The route passing through this gateway, and to faith, is the heart. But first we must open the gate. Pascal's skepticism served to highlight the limits of reason and experience, rather than to show that we lack knowledge. And like Descartes, Pascal was willing to entertain the most radical skeptical ideas, including that reason and experience on their own cannot show much about even ordinary objects in the external world or the basic principles of geometry. In some ways, he went even further down the skeptic's rabbit-hole. But his point was not to cast doubt on those first principles or the objects of our senses, but rather to emphasize that, when we know about the world – that it is not all just a long dream, whether there is a creator, what are the principles of geometry, and even how to understand our most basic concepts – it is not merely through reason and the senses. Rather, such knowledge depends on "the heart," which is the seat of affect and the will, and operates by the grace of an external force. Try as you might, the heart must be moved by something outside of the individual, and it is in virtue of this – not just reason – that we know anything. Pascal's epistemology is in this sense anti-individualist: the possibility of all meaningful knowledge depends on the grace of something external to us. There is a way to read that in which it is trivial: whatever it is you know about the world, the world has to be that way (and arguably has to be causally involved in your believing that it is that way). But Pascal's view is more radical: if human reason (and experience) operates on its own in the world, it cannot know the world.

The insufficiency of our individual faculties of reason and experience, and our tendency to mistakenly think that these are all we need, is part of a larger picture Pascal has of human nature: on its own, it is corrupt and hopeless. It is presumptuous, as is typical of us, to think we can go it alone. But there is a silver lining: reason itself can show us this insufficiency, and we see our limitations enough to aspire to transcend them. So while reason cannot by itself tell us much about the world with any certainty, it can delineate its own limits, and that is a major step towards what Pascal would call "salvation." Another way to put it, though, is that reason, while insufficient to establish the nature of the world, is sufficient to establish our own deficiencies, and to tell us what kind of intervention would be necessary for us to know the nature of the world. Moreover, the fact that reason and experience cannot themselves show us the true nature of things also corroborates (in a sense to be explained further) Christianity uniquely among the religions and philosophies of the world. This is an important point for Pascal, but it is also suggestive of a more general idea. Any view of reality and humanity's place within it must accommodate the fact that reason and experience are insufficient in the ways that Pascal has shown. And, relatedly, any such worldview must accommodate the fact (at least as Pascal claims) that our faculties *plus* the right kind of external inspiration *do* make the true nature of the world manifest. It is not possible to see this grand Pascalian scheme, though, without first understanding the limits of our own, individual faculties of reason and experience. One major upshot will be that the way the world appears, and therefore what it is reasonable for us to surmise about it, depends on our basic orientation, the state of one's heart. This itself is a substantive fact about the world.

It should be acknowledged that the basic strategy of motivating faith by appealing to skepticism was familiar in Pascal's day and is not itself unique or original. In fact, it can be found not only in his direct precursors like Montaigne (and Charron), but in Scripture itself, which he quotes in Latin:

> Quod ergo ignorantes, quæritis, religio annuntiat vobis (Acts 17:23)
>
> (What you seek in ignorance religion announces to you)

He quotes this in a note suggesting that skepticism is both true and in service to religion:

> Skepticism is the truth. For, after all, men before Jesus Christ did not know where they stood, nor if they were great or small. And those who said one or the other knew nothing about it, and guessed without reason and by chance, and indeed they always erred by excluding the one or the other. (S570/L691)

But Pascal plots a unique course from skepticism to a religious apology, via his epistemology, and what he has in mind with the "great" and the "small" is entirely original.

The idea that our reason itself does not produce indubitable conclusions might sound outlandish to some. To those familiar with the most famous early modern philosophers, including Descartes (Pascal's contemporary) and Hume, it will seem more familiar. It is a good place to start exploring the skeptical side of Pascal's thought because it is both radical and clear. We will begin by trying to get to the bottom of geometry. The geometrical style of proof, which was also put on a pedestal in Descartes' philosophy, is according to Pascal the source of our greatest degree of certainty. But even here, where reason seems most comfortably at home, reason does not provide for the fundamentals.

1.1 Geometry, Space, and Spatial Infinities

Let us start with Pascal's view of the geometrical method outlined in two essays, *The Geometrical Mind* and *The Art of Persuasion*, before moving on to his remarks on this in the *Pensées*.[1] That which provides certainty in geometry in the first place is, in *The Geometrical Mind*,

---

[1] For these two essays, I borrow translations and cite page numbers from Richard Popkin's *Pascal: Selections* (Macmillan, 1989).

nature or our natural instinct. But we see in *The Art of Persuasion* that the will, and not just reason or the mind, is often the basis of what we believe, and this explains why we disagree with others and with ourselves at different times. We see in both essays ideas that are then further elaborated in the *Pensées*, so we know that these are consistent elements of Pascal's thought. Natural instinct in *The Geometrical Mind* and the idea that the will is responsible for belief, in general and most importantly religion, are elaborated and developed, and assimilated in the *Pensées* into "the heart."

In *The Geometrical Mind*, Pascal sets out to explain how we can provide a proof for something that we already believe, and makes two main points. The first is that we cannot define our most basic notions, such as "space," "time," "whole," and even "being," in any terms that are clearer than those very notions. Geometry is as good a way to think as is possible for humankind precisely because it does not try to define its basic terms. Rather, it takes them as a conceptual starting point and then defines all other, less basic terms on that basis. The second main point in the essay is that every proof has some premises, and each premise can in principle be queried, so that one can always search for a proof of that premise. Since we are finite, this cannot go on forever. But some premises are so natural and obvious, and so widely accepted, that there is no possible proof of them whose premises are more certain than they are. Just as some basic concepts are naturally clearer than any others with which you might define them, some premises are naturally more plausible than any other with which you might prove them. Nature, when it comes to our basic concepts and first principles, provides us with a starting point for geometry. In fact, Pascal notes that those who try to define those basic terms or try to prove first principles, descend into nonsense. So quickly can you go from engaging in the most perfect use of reason to the most ridiculous and useless. The first principles are at our foundation, "Nature sustaining it for want of reasoning," (176) he writes. In geometry, these natural first principles include things such as that any quantity or extension can be doubled, and that any quantity or extension is divisible. Our most basic commitments (axioms, definitions) are not derivable, and it is taken for granted, at this stage, that as nature, not an individual's reason, determines these starting points, in this respect, all of us share the same nature.

This sort of foundationalist view will be familiar to readers of Descartes, who makes a similar appeal to "the natural light" (or clear and distinct perception), and one can also find in it a precursor to the commonsense philosophy of G. E. Moore. But we will soon see that the way in which nature operates to determine our starting points, and the fact that we are capable of having different natures, will make for a unique and powerful epistemology when it comes to other subject matter, beyond geometry.

So far, though, none of this sounds terribly "skeptical." Sure, our reason has limits even in geometry, but whoever would have expected otherwise? We are limited beings. The *ideal* method, as Pascal notes at the outset, would be one by which all terms are defined, and all premises proved, but this would require a superhuman, infinite mind that can keep offering definitions and justifications an infinite number of times. Within our limits, geometry with its natural foundations or starting points, is as good as it gets. But here already we have the seed of a more troubling thought. Just *how* limited are we, how far away from that infinite, impossible mind? We cannot even understand what such a mind would be. And if we cannot prove that which nature determines is our foundation, how do we know these foundational principles are true? It seems there is no reason to think they are not wrong. And if we just accept them, they still lead to troubling questions. We are given that all things are infinitely divisible, and infinitely multipliable, for example. So we understand that in principle things could be infinitely larger than us, or infinitely smaller.

Where, then, are we? Look at your hand. What magnitude is this hand, if it is both infinitely smaller and infinitely larger than what *could* be in existence? How can you have an idea of how large or small anything is, including yourself, if you have no idea of how large or small the rest of reality is? Mighty giant or just a mite? Pascal calls this "the two marvelous infinities that [nature] has set forth for men, not to conceive, but to admire" (184). So even our natural foundations present us with cause for, if not yet skepticism, humility. Later, in the *Pensées*, he will meditate on these two infinites more comprehensively, with respect to the significance of human life in general (not just its physical dimension). We leave *The Geometrical Mind*, however, wondering why nature furnished us with the starting points of reason that it did. Could we have had different starting points? Are these starting points just useful, or convenient, or are they actually true?² It is also worth noticing that reason, though it did not furnish us with a foundation itself, at least was able to show that there is a foundation, and in doing so delineates its own limit. These are all ideas that Pascal takes up in the more explicitly skeptical fragments of the *Pensées*.

In *The Art of Persuasion*, Pascal considers how to convince someone of something they don't already believe. Here, he notes that reasoning is not the only source of belief, so persuasion can't consist solely in reasoning. In fact, we usually don't even try to prove what we believe: "all men are almost always led to believe not by proof, but by pleasures [l'agrément]" (186). This is, he says in the current context, "base" and "unworthy," and people generally disapprove of it, even though almost all of us do it.

Some things to note here. Pascal generally looks down on the fact that we tend to believe what we find agreeable, or what satisfies our pleasure. This is an instance of a general tendency in Pascal to think of what we love and want, or the will, as typically *corrupting*. The way in which our desires and fears can warp our path to belief was familiar to philosophers of his day, to the ancients, and also to contemporary philosophers and psychologists today who call this "motivated reasoning." When we see an opportunity to believe something we want to believe, because it is convenient given our other attitudes and commitments, we will accept evidence for it easily, and will criticize evidence against it and resist as much as we can.³

---

² It seems that some physicists today believe that Pascal's examples of first principles are false, because they no longer take space to be Euclidian, or they hold that space is unbounded but not infinite. It isn't obvious how exactly Pascal would have handled these contemporary developments, but it seems clear he would not resist them. Pascal never says we have any guarantee that nature has given us *true* foundations, and he certainly thought that nature has sometimes endowed us with corrupt, rather than perfect features and intuitions. Moreover, as we will see next, in the second essay, *The Art of Persuasion*, Pascal explains not only how error is possible, but how we can come to see things differently from how we currently see them, even when it comes to the foundations.

³ Francis Bacon was another seventeenth-century thinker who anticipated this important idea, in 1620 in his *Novum Organum:* "The human understanding is no dry light, but receives an infusion from the will and affections; whence proceed sciences which may be called 'sciences as one would.' For what a man had rather were true he more readily believes ... Numberless, in short, are the ways, and sometimes imperceptible, in which the affections color and infect the understanding." In the twentieth century, Ziva Kunda (most famously in Kunda, Ziva (1990).

1.1 Geometry, Space, and Spatial Infinities

The result is that we are generally more likely to believe what we are independently motivated to believe by our hearts and wills. This not only makes us unreliable, since as far as we know what we want has no automatic correlation to the truth, but also easy to manipulate. For example, your online news feed and the news you get on social media is filled with content that an algorithm has placed there because of your antecedent interests, desires and fears, or that your friends, who are likely to agree in many of your attitudes, saw fit to post. And so you are invited by your devices, constantly, to confirm and take on beliefs that are consonant with your attitudes, even those that have nothing to do with reality. Pascal is here noticing a fact about us as believers that not only cuts deep, but that makes us especially susceptible to manipulation *today* given current technology and the way most of us get our information online. He goes on in this essay, and in similar passages in the *Pensées* which we will soon examine, to explain how one must appeal to a person's desires and fears, and not just their reason, to persuade them of something new.

However, when he disavows the influence of our desires on our beliefs as unworthy, he immediately makes an exception: faith. Some things "must be loved in order to be known" and these things are within a "supernatural order, completely contrary to the order which ought to be natural to men in natural matters." The problem is that our desires do not belong in the belief-forming mechanism of the lower, natural or physical order of humankind, but since we are corrupt, our desires operate there too (186). For Pascal, the correct method of belief when it comes to nonreligious matters is modeled on the geometrical method. But, unlike Descartes, Pascal does not think reason is capable of application to loftier things, for example, God and the big picture questions *about* the natural order of things. And we've seen that reason is also not up to the task of supporting the foundations of geometrical thinking. Reason has its limits clearly delineated here.

Crucially, the correct method when it comes to the higher, divine order of things *must* involve our desires or the will. In *The Art of Persuasion*, Pascal offers just a brief explanation: when it comes to divine

---

The case for motivated reasoning. *Psychological Bulletin* 108, 480–498) developed a research program to study this phenomenon and named it "motivated reasoning," a major topic of study in psychology and philosophy today.

things, you must first love in order to understand. (This is a classic Augustinian principle, from *De Trinitate* (8.5.8), inspired by Isaiah Vii, 9, "Unless you believe, you will not understand."[4] The idea is that first you have faith in God, and only then can you understand God.) Love comes first, before understanding and belief, as it properly should when it comes to supernatural things, but not physical or mundane and natural ones. One must, if one wants to understand supernatural things, "subdue the rebellion of the will by an entirely celestial sweetness which charms it and transports it" (186). Something entirely distinct from you, and outside of your control, has to seduce you first.[5] We can glean from all of this the idea that, if one's beliefs (or lack of belief) are problematic, the answer is not necessarily to bombard one with proofs and reasoned arguments. The root of the problem may well be in one's heart.

How do we reach someone's heart? How do we know our own heart is in the right place? And can the state of one's heart, the will that goes on to condition belief, be evaluated in the same way as the state of one's beliefs, that is, for how true or correct it is? We cannot answer these questions, or see how they are pressing today as ever, until we get a better idea of the limits of reason and the corresponding role of "the heart." That role depends on exactly the contours of the heart-shaped, or cordate hole that is left when our reason can go no further.

And so already, before even beginning to look at the *Pensées*, we can see that Pascal is not quite a rationalist in any straightforward sense. We *feel* (*sent* in French), somehow, with our hearts that the foundational things are certain, and this capacity to feel is sometimes misplaced and corrupts our reasoning process.

In the *Pensées* we see the limits of reason emphasized again, though here it is presented explicitly as a *skeptical* (sometimes "Pyrrhonian") point and applied more broadly, beyond just geometrical first principles. In every case, reason and experience do not by themselves deliver

---

[4] This famous line is arguably mistranslated, but has taken on theological significance of its own. Robert Alter's recent translation seems more accurate: "If you trust not, you shall not hold firm." He speculates: "[I]t probably means that if Ahaz does not trust Isaiah and hold out against Rezin and Pekah, he will come to a bad end" Alter, Robert (2019). Isaiah. In *The Hebrew Bible: A Translation with Commentary* (complete Tanakh edition). New York: W. W. Norton & Company.
[5] Pascal makes much the same point in the fourth letter to Roannes.

the goods. The two fragments in the *Pensées* that most directly and thoroughly lay out Pascal's views here are S142/L110 and S164/L131. The former begins by confirming the skeptical view about first principles:

> We know the truth, not only through reason, but also through the heart. It is through the latter that we know first principles. ... For knowledge of first principles, such as space, time, motion, number, [is] as firm as any we derive from reasoning. Reason must use this knowledge from the heart and instinct, and base all its arguments on it. The heart feels that there are three dimensions in space and numbers are infinite, and reason then shows that there are no two square numbers of which one is double the other. Principles are felt, propositions are proved; all with certainty, though in different ways. And it is as useless and absurd for reason to demand from the heart proofs of its first principles before accepting them, as it would be for the heart to demand from reason an intuition of all demonstrated propositions before receiving them. This inability must serve, then, only to humble reason, which would want to be judge of everything, but not to attack our certainty. As if reason alone were capable of teaching us! Would to God, on the contrary, that we never had need of it, and that we knew everything by instinct and intuition, But nature has refused us this good, giving us instead very little knowledge of this kind. And all other knowledge can be acquired only by reasoning.

And the latter fragment makes more explicit the skeptical upshot:

> The most powerful argument of the skeptics ... is that we have no certainty of the truth of these principles (apart from faith and revelation), except insofar as we naturally perceive them in ourselves. Now, this natural sensation is not a convincing proof of their truth. There is no certainty, apart from faith, as to whether man was created by a good God, by an evil demon, or by chance, so depending on our origin, it is doubtful whether these principles given to us are true, or false, or uncertain. (S164/L131)

This seems like a reference to, and a departure from, Descartes' position. According to Descartes, the "natural light" or "intuition" can *prove* the existence of a benevolent God, who would not place in us a natural faculty that leads us astray. Instead, for Pascal, this is a matter of faith and revelation, not proof. And God *did* place in us some faculties that lead us astray! (The reason God did this is explained by the Fall, which I discuss further.) Proofs such as the ontological argument (which Descartes appeals to) are among the "metaphysical proofs" of God's existence, which Pascal also downplays (at best). The present point, though, is that it is through faith, and not through reason, that we know things on the basis of our natural faculties. And this faith is put in us thanks to something external to ourselves: nature. The mere fact that nature gave us the first principles it did is no reason, itself, to think that these first principles are true. So, insofar as it occurs to us to doubt our faith, we do seem to be confronted with a skeptical problem, since nothing else can shore up our foundations. Next, Pascal applies a similar thought to our sensory faculties and our knowledge of external things.

1.2 Dreams and the "External World"

Continuing S142/L110 and S164/L131, we see a similar move made about the possibility that you are now dreaming, a topic also familiar from Descartes' *Meditations*. That you may be dreaming, and that this undermines your certainty about the world as presented through your senses, is of course a mainstay of contemporary debates about skepticism as well. This is how Pascal approaches it in S164/L131:

> [N]o person has any certainty, apart from faith, whether he is awake or asleep, seeing that during sleep we believe we are awake as firmly as we are now. We believe we see spaces, shapes, and motions. We feel the passing of time, we measure it, and in fact we behave as we do when we are awake. Given that half of our life is spent in sleep, we have by our own admission no idea of truth, whatever we may imagine. All our sensations, then, are simply illusions. Who knows whether this other half of our life, in which we think we are awake, is not another sleep slightly different from the first half, from which we awake when we think we are asleep? Since we often dream that we are dreaming, piling up dream upon dream, it could well be that this half of our life, in which we think we are awake, is itself only a dream on which the others are grafted and from which we awaken at death. During this state we have as few principles of truth and good as we have during natural sleep; this flowing of time and life, these various bodies we feel, these different thoughts disturbing us are perhaps only illusions similar to the passage of time and the vain phantoms of our dreams.

At the end of the *Meditations*, Descartes famously remarks that there is a coherence to our waking life, that we have memories of past days in

1.2 *Dreams and the "External World"* 23

which we were awake, and that this indicates, given that there is a non-deceiving God who would not trick us, that we are not dreaming. Pascal's idea that what we call waking life could, for all reason can prove, be like one long dream on which smaller dreams are grafted (so that in the long dream we dream that we go to sleep), seems to be a good rebuttal to this, and it seems to present us with a more radical skeptical challenge than the typical dreaming scenario. It is one thing to ask how we know we are not now dreaming the sort of dream we remember ourselves often having while asleep; it is another thing to ask how we know that all of what we think of as waking life is not *like* a nightly dream, and that we have never yet been awake, in the sense of being sensorily in contact with reality. Just as there might be some coherence and inner connections within a regular dream – you can remember later in the dream what you did earlier in the dream – there is coherence in the *long* dream that is your whole life. But it's still all a dream, none of what your senses present is really happening. If so, you've never experienced waking before, you've only falsely dreamt awakenings. You've never been truly awake, you've only dreamed that you've been awake, as part of the long dream. This seems a more difficult challenge than Descartes' because the qualities we use to distinguish dreams from waking, such as the coherence and memory connections that Descartes appeals to, may simply be qualities that the long dream has.

To be fair, Descartes *did* have an ace up his sleeve, the proof of a non-deceiving God's existence, and we have not yet covered why Pascal rejects such proofs. Pascal's point is limited to the idea that it is not enough to say that things are not happening now in the disjointed way typical of dreaming during the night, and that currently you are enjoying a consistent and coherent connection, through memory, of past waking moments. To say this is to not yet to rule out Pascal's *long* dream, with smaller dreams grafted onto it. Such a long dream would feel just like this – coherence, memory and all – so even a non-deceiving God isn't on the hook for guaranteeing you are not in Pascal's long dream. A non-deceiving God, if He wanted to make it seem to you like you are in Pascal's long dream, would give you experience *just like the ones you are having now*.

Consider that possibility. A non-deceiving God might, for all we know, want you to have a long dream throughout your "life," and wake you to finally and for the first time experience reality only in your heavenly afterlife.[6] Perhaps this would make your suffering, and your bad decisions in "life," less significant, if it all took place in a long dream – we all *feel* life's agonies are really happening, but we will eventually wake up and understand these were empty sensations. Remarkably, Pascal not only rejects the idea that proof of a non-deceiving God shows that we are not in this situation but he also explicitly rejects any such implications about our suffering. Life as one long dream would be equivalent to our current lives, not only in experience but also in our suffering and its significance:

> If we dreamed the same thing every night, it would affect us as much as the objects we see every day. And if an artisan were sure to dream every night for twelve hours that he was a king, I believe he would be almost as happy as a king who dreamed every night for twelve hours that he was an artisan.
>
> If we dreamed every night that we were pursued by enemies and harassed by these painful phantoms, or that we spent every day in different occupations, as when traveling, we would suffer almost as much as if it were real, and would dread going to sleep, as we dread waking up when we are afraid in fact to encounter such mishaps. And, indeed, this would cause pretty much the same discomforts as reality.
>
> But since dreams are all different, and even each is varied, what we see in them affects us much less than what we see when we are awake, because of the continuity, which is not, however, so continuous and even as not to change too, though less abruptly, even if rarely, as when we travel; and then we say: it seems to me I am dreaming. For life is a dream, a little less unstable. (S653/L803)

When it comes to our happiness or misery – a topic about which Pascal had a lot to say – the long dream is *irrelevant*. We cannot find our moral compass, or the measure of our life's happiness, by determining whether it is "really happening." And this is because, fundamentally, our unhappiness is the result of our own, inner orientation, the state of our hearts. One reason to dismiss the long dream possibility is that it makes no

---

[6] Al-Ghazali's *Deliverance from Error* predates (by several centuries) and anticipates much of this dialectic, in both Descartes and Pascal. In paragraph 14, he attributes to the Prophet Muhammad the claim that dying is like waking up for the first time.

1.2 Dreams and the "External World"

difference to our hearts, or to how our life is going. It is therefore hard to take such possibilities very seriously.

At any rate, what is needed to confront the challenge that life might be a long dream is faith, according to Pascal. It is clear that he thinks we *do* know that life is really happening, that we are not dreaming:

> We know we are not dreaming, however powerless we are to prove it by reason. This inability demonstrates only the weakness of our reason, and not, as they claim, the uncertainty of all our knowledge. (S142/L110)

The lesson, then, is *not* that the skeptic wins. It's not that you don't know whether life is but a dream. You *do* know that life is not a dream. But you don't know it through proving anything, through the use of your reason or experience. You know it by faith, which is to say by the heart. This means something like: you feel that this is real, you don't prove that this is real. Life is not about proving things, it is about feeling the right things. We should try to feel correctly.

However, feeling that this is not a dream is not optional, so there is nothing to feeling correctly in this respect. The feeling that this is real, and not one long dream, is inescapable. In fact, Pascal anticipates Hume (this reflects the influence on both of them of the ancient skeptics, but also the fact that Hume read Pascal) and notes that skepticism is useless because *nature* makes it so.[7] For example, just after he describes our incapacity to defeat skepticism by the use of reason, in S164/L131, Pascal writes:

> I pause at the dogmatists' [the anti-skeptics] only strong point, which is that, speaking in good faith and sincerely, we cannot doubt natural principles. ... What then shall man do in this state? Shall he doubt everything? Doubt whether he is awake, whether he is being pinched, whether he is being burned? Doubt whether he doubts? Doubt whether he exists? We cannot go that far, and I advance as fact that there never has been a fully effective skeptic. Nature sustains our feeble reason and prevents it from ranting so wildly. Shall he then say, on the contrary, that he certainly has the truth, when at the slightest pressure he can produce no evidence for it and is forced to let go of his grasp?

---

[7] There is a large literature on this topic in Hume (usually termed Hume's "naturalism"). For my own take on what Hume thought about our natures and skepticism, see Avnur, Yuval (2015). Excuses for Hume's Skepticism. *Philosophy and Phenomenological Research* 92 (2): 264–306.

> Know then, proud man, what a paradox you are to yourself. Humble yourself, powerless reason; be silent, dumb nature; learn that man infinitely transcends man, and hear from your Master your true condition, of which you are ignorant.
> Listen to God.

Here we get the upshots of all of Pascal's skeptical musings. As we've seen, we cannot prove that we are not dreaming, or that an evil demon is not tricking us every time we are naturally certain about a first principle. So we must put reason in its place. It does not secure the foundations of our beliefs. But this cannot lead us to doubt, because where reason fails to establish foundations, nature makes the foundations indubitable. This is so despite the fact that we have no proof that justifies these foundations. Nor, we have seen, does this imply that we don't *know* the things we take ourselves to know: that we are awake, that 2 + 2 = 4, and that any quantity or distance can be multiplied infinitely. We know this only because there is something external to us, and beyond our ken, that gives us this knowledge. Something made us naturally feel that this is reality, and not a dream: God. We are entirely epistemically dependent on God. It is important to emphasize, though, that God does not provide this knowledge because we can, with the correct use of reason, prove that God is a non-deceiver, a la Descartes. No, we are a *paradox* to ourselves. This is what skeptical reasoning shows us, that in our current state we cannot make sense of ourselves, let alone of how or why God does whatever He does or why nature is the way it is. This is one role that God plays in Pascalian epistemology: giving us knowledge where reason cannot, because we make no sense to ourselves. And God plays this role through faith and the heart, though it remains for us to see how this works.

Importantly, it is not, though, that faith plays a role that *contradicts* reason and experience:

> Faith truly says what the senses do not say, but not the contrary of what they see. It is above, not against them. (S217/L185)

This is an important point, because – as we will see again and again – Pascal's God does not ask us for *blind* faith, to believe contradictions, or to go against what we see.

We have already seen Pascal suggest that our *hearts* feel first principles, so that the astute reader will have already connected the role of God and the role of the heart in Pascal's epistemological outlook, since the heart is the seat of faith. One could say, then, that on Pascal's view, our hearts are faithful to this life being real, not a dream. It isn't clear why, but again it seems plausible enough that we are all like this, or that it is only thanks to the heart that we can take our experience of the world to be veridical. Setting God aside for a moment, what many of us want to say is that, though we recognize that it's a technical possibility that this is all a dream, we can't really believe it. And though maybe some philosopher somewhere can claim to prove somehow that we are not dreaming, and not deceived by a demon, and so on, even if we can see such proofs as convincing for a while, we don't really rest our belief that this is reality, and not a dream, on *that*. Most people are not aware of such proofs, and those who are do not agree about whether they work, or which one works. Nor, I think, does the idea that nature just made us this way constitute any reason or proof. For one, it doesn't seem generally true: a disturbed human might come to doubt whether this is not a long dream. In fact, some religious believers might think just that! Perhaps life is not real, it is all a test, and we engage reality only when we make it to the afterlife. Nature didn't make these possibilities *impossible* to believe. And even if it did, how does this help us make sense of ourselves or justify our faith that this is reality? Couldn't nature have simply disposed us toward a false belief? This is indeed what we see in many other domains: it is natural to think that the earth is flat if one simply looks around, to commit the gamblers fallacy, and so on.[8] All of these reflections seem reasonable enough, and they are the skeptical upshot of Pascal's view of things. At bottom, we take this life to be real because we just overwhelmingly feel that it's real; as a spider just knows how to weave a web, humans just know how to form beliefs on the basis of their sense experiences during waking life, and thus they feel they are awake.

Let us pause to take stock. Nature – or the natural state of our heart – makes it practically impossible to be skeptics; reason makes it impossible

---

[8] The classic study on the gambler's fallacy is Tversky, Amos, & Kahneman, Daniel (1971). Belief in the law of small numbers. *Psychological Bulletin* 76 (2): 105–110.

to be "dogmatists" (those who insist that we can know, by reason, the things we typically take ourselves to know, such as that we are not now dreaming). Humans seem stuck here, lost. But Pascal went even further. He innovated another, perhaps even more radical way of showing that we are lost and articulating our lostness. Nature furnishes us with certain basic concepts and first principles that are not themselves provable by reason. But reason not only cannot prove those first principles, it also positively establishes a space for us to become lost. This is an existential application of the two infinities we encountered in our discussion of geometry. And this time, nature does not determine for us what to think, only your individual heart can do that.

1.3 Lost between Two Infinities

Pascal realized that not only do we depend on something outside of reason to establish our basic relation to reality and not only does this imply that we cannot make sense of ourselves as creatures of *reason* only, but this situation also opens unlimited possibilities for what we could be and the significance of our lives. Reason's limitation gives our imagination free reign to explore the possible extent of reality, which not only produces a sense of wonder but also makes it impossible to measure ourselves within reality. Pascal found this terrifying, which takes skepticism a further step in a metaphysical and existential direction. Not only are we unable (without faith) to determine our relation to reality in the sense of whether we are in contact with it but we are also unable to determine how important or significant we are – though these amount to different problems depending on the kind of significance we have in mind. The imagination, unconstrained by any limits determined by reason, runs free and loses itself.

This idea, that we cannot determine our own significance in the universe, is found in numerous parts of Pascal's writings, but it is most thoroughly explained and explored in a fragment entitled "The disproportion of man," S230/L199. It begins like this:

> Here is where natural knowledge leads us: if it is not true, there is no truth in man; and if it is true, he finds in it a great source of humiliation, forced to humble himself one way or another.

1.3 Lost between Two Infinities

We found this thought already in *The Geometrical Mind*, that "natural knowledge" or knowledge on the basis of our natural capacities, leads us to conclude that what we believe may turn out to be false ("no truth"), and even if the principles we naturally find compelling are true, these principles "humble us" because they suggest that we could be miniscule and insignificant. How so? He has in mind the fact that we naturally accept that any quantity, and any spatial expanse, could be doubled, tripled, and so on. And likewise, spatial expanses can be halved, and halved again, and so on. But rather than stick to abstract geometry, Pascal here describes how everything – the earth, the other planets, the sun, the stars – is just tiny specks compared to what can be conceived beyond that in the universe as a whole, and that nothing we imagine, however great, is anything but a mere speck of still larger things:

> However much we may inflate our conceptions beyond these imaginable spaces, we give birth only to atoms with respect to the reality of things.

Reality, as far as our natural knowledge tells us, "is an infinite sphere whose center is everywhere and circumference nowhere."[9]

Any large, amazing thing like a galaxy or nebula can be imagined as a tiny speck within a yet larger world. Perhaps the entire universe, which scientists tell us today originated in a big bang, is a singularity within a black hole of a yet larger universe. How could there ever be *empirical* evidence for or against this? (Recall, our experience doesn't even tell us whether this is all a dream!) The point here is that our imagination is unconstrained from thinking it is so, because our reason impels our notion of *even larger* onward. The universe can get bigger and bigger without contradicting anything we know to be true. Not only are we infinitely tiny compared to what we can image the universe to be, we also have no idea of our place within this infinite expanse. The center of an infinite sphere is "everywhere." So, what is our significance in this picture? "What is a man in the infinite?"

> Let him lose himself in wonders as astonishing in their minuteness as the others are in their extent! For who will not marvel that our body, imperceptible a little while ago in the universe, itself imperceptible inside

---

[9] This is the line that inspired Jorge Luis Borges' fascinating essay, The Fearful Sphere of Pascal, in *Labyrinths: Selected Stories & Other Writings*. New Directions Pub. Corp, 1964.

the totality, should now be a colossus, a world, or rather a whole, with respect to the nothingness beyond our reach?

Just as we are practically nothing in the largeness of the universe, we are also giants, or an entire world, compared to how tiny things can be and certainly compared to nothingness. In a little speck of dust, we can imagine tinier and tinier specks and things, parts of that speck of dust, and things can get infinitely smaller, perhaps. And there is no number of times you could multiply *nothing* to get to any positive size at all. The universe as a whole is unimaginably large, and each little part of it, let alone nothingness, is unimaginably small. You, a human, are colossal compared to the tininess of things. So we are both infinitely small (compared to the whole) and infinitely large (compared to the parts):

> For, in the end, what is man in nature? A nothing compared to the infinite, an everything compared to the nothing, a midpoint between nothing and everything, infinitely removed from understanding the extremes: the end of things and their principle are hopelessly hidden from him in an impenetrable secret. What then will he be able to conceive? He is equally incapable of seeing the nothingness from which he derives and the infinite in which he is engulfed.

When we compare the question "what is man in nature?" with some other fragments, it appears that Pascal tried to develop this thought, that we are lost and cannot find ourselves, from a number of angles. For example, he considers that every person, regardless of their station in life, cannot find any a solid indication of how life is going, because the way one's life is going is due to seemingly arbitrary and contingent factors which, as far as one can tell by one's own capacities and reason, just happened to be that way. One cannot, then, make sense of one's life based on how it is going and who one is in society.[10] He makes a similar move with respect to our position in *time* and the duration of our lifetime. It is put so beautifully (and readers of the Bible will recognize an allusion to Ecclesiastes) that it is worth quoting here:

> When I consider the brief duration of my life absorbed in the eternity that lies before and after – The memory of a guest who stays only a day –

---

[10] See for example L194/S227, L198/S229, and an essay we haven't mentioned, *Three Discourses on the Condition of the Great*.

1.3 Lost between Two Infinities

> the small space I occupy and can even see, engulfed in the infinite immensity of spaces I do not know and that do not know me, I am frightened and astonished to see myself here rather than there; for there is no reason why I am here rather than there, why now rather than then. Who put me here? By whose order and direction have this place and time been allotted to me? (S102/L68)[11]

In S55/L21, he makes a similar point about perspective: we become lost in the sense of not knowing how our current perspective compares with others, and which one (if any) is the most correct. This is Pascal taking the classic skeptical thought and applying it in fascinating and creative ways. And once again we see that, despite the fragmentary appearance of Pascal's writing as we see it today, there was a sustained effort to make sense of the main ideas in a systematic way. That our own capacity to understand the world and ourselves leaves us totally lost is explored from every angle: time, space, and circumstance.

The sense in which we are lost because we cannot use a maximum or minimum size for any reference point is literal. You cannot know where you are and what you are *in space* if things can get infinitely larger or smaller. One almost wants to say: then there is no size, no location, which is one way to take Pascal's remark that the center is everywhere. The contingency of happening to be "here" rather than "there," and the time in which one finds oneself, conveys a different sense of lostness: lost in time and lacking any sense of why one is where and when one is, lacking explanation of one's circumstances. The arbitrariness of one's perspective conveys yet another way of being lost: am I seeing the world clearly and correctly? What is the actual angle of things?

Pascal goes on to explore another sense of lostness. In the main fragment that we are currently exploring, he applies the idea that things can go infinitely on in either direction a bit more abstractly, to our intellectual capacity:

> Let us, then, understand our condition: we are something and we are not everything. Such being as we have removes us from knowledge of first principles, which arise out of nothingness. And the smallness of our being conceals from us the sight of the infinite. Our intellect holds the

---

[11] For a recent classic dealing with similar questions, see Nagel, Thomas (1971). The absurd. *Journal of Philosophy* 68 (20): 716–727.

same rank in the order of intelligible things as our body occupies in the extension of nature.

Just as we cannot find our *physical* position, we cannot find our *intellectual* place within nature, when we imagine that understanding can itself be miniscule or complete. This is because we don't know how deep the principles that our natural reason can perceive go, whether there are further principles that explain them that are unintelligible to us. In some ways, this latter point about our intellect is the larger problem. We know *something* about reality, but because we don't know how much about reality we really know, we don't know the significance of, or the measure of, this knowledge. It could be a mere speck of knowledge, it could be almost everything there is to know.

> This is our true state. It is what makes us incapable of certain knowledge or absolute ignorance. We float on a vast ocean, ever uncertain and adrift, blown this way or that. . . . We burn with desire to find firm ground and an ultimate secure base on which to build a tower reaching up to the infinite. But our whole foundation cracks, and the earth opens up into abysses.

And here is an important implication:

> Our reason is always deceived by inconstant appearances; nothing can affix the finite between the two infinites that both enclose and escape it.

He calls this "the proof of our weakness." So we see that his skeptical considerations, which place limits on what we can naturally know through reason and experience, also open up limitless possibilities for what reality could be, and for what our place in it could be. But this is not merely supposed to fill you with amazement and wonder at the possibilities. It is supposed to fill you with existential terror: what is the measure of humankind? What is your place – spatially, temporally, and *intellectually* – in the universe? As he puts it in a different fragment, "[t]he eternal silence of these infinite spaces frightens me" (S233/L201).

As Moriarty vividly puts it, what the two infinities fragment does is "establish humankind's quantitative incommensurability with the cosmos."[12] We know that we understand more than a rock, say. Maybe we

---

[12] Moriarty, Michael (2020). Pascal: Reasoning and Belief. Oxford University Press. (p. 312)

1.3 Lost between Two Infinities 33

understand more than a simple creature, a worm. But since "[o]ur intellect holds the same rank in the order of intelligible things as our body occupies in the extension of nature," we don't know whether we are almost totally ignorant, or almost totally omniscient in our understanding of nature compared to what it is possible to understand.

This observation hits home especially today. What is the human understanding of reality compared to a new and sophisticated artificial intelligence, or an alien somewhere out there in space? Is there that much more for it to know than what we can know? Or could it know only more of the same kind of thing as we do, perhaps just faster or a greater quantity of it? How close to final is our understanding? We cannot fathom what there is beyond our understanding, because we cannot transcend ourselves – not, at least, by our natural knowledge of things by reason. Consider, even, whether just as consciousness seems completely transcendent beyond unconsciousness (a mind versus a pebble), there could be something that is just as transcendent beyond consciousness. We could not understand such a thing, any more than a pebble can understand a mind, but we also can't rule it out. We don't know the significance of our *size* because the universe could be infinitely vast, and could be made up of infinitely small parts. But we also don't know the extent of our understanding, in just the same way; if there is much better or more understanding possible, then what we do understand is of little value, intellectually. The result is that human reason and understanding, as well as human life itself, is lost, immeasurable, and humbled.

This can all be seen as part of Pascal's skeptical outlook, which implies not only ignorance about what reality is (e.g., whether this is all a long dream) but also *what we are*. This is an often overlooked aspect of even standard skeptical arguments more familiar from today's philosophy. It is often remarked that we cannot know whether we are victims of *The Matrix*, brains floating in a vat, and so on. But if we cannot know that, how do we know what we are? As the classical Chinese philosopher Chuang-Zi once mused, just as you can dream that you are a butterfly, perhaps you are currently a butterfly dreaming that you are a human. The great logician Kurt Gödel, in a letter of August 12, 1961, points out the same crucial question, which is too often overlooked: "We not only don't even know whence and why we are here, but also don't know what we are (namely, in essence and seen from within)."¹³ These questions were not lost on Pascal, whereas the standard epistemological picture tends to miss them. His meditation on the two infinities, in its various forms, articulates the relation between skepticism about the external world and skepticism about what we are.

But Pascal follows all of this up on a more optimistic note, about our dignity despite all this. Here he focuses on our measure compared to the physical universe, or nature as we know it. Recall that we are somewhere between nothing and everything, so we are something. What kind of something are we? We are extremely weak compared to nature, but we are greater than it still. This is expressed in his "thinking reed" metaphor:

> Man is only a reed, the weakest thing in nature, but he is a thinking reed. The whole universe does not need to take up arms to crush him; a vapor, a drop of water, is enough to kill him. But if the universe were to crush him, man would still be nobler than what killed him, because he knows he is dying and the advantage the universe has over him. The universe knows nothing of this. (S231/L200)

As he puts it elsewhere,

> [t]hrough space the universe encompasses and swallows me up like a mere point, through thought I encompass it. (S145/L113)

Although we are lost in the physical universe, the fact that we can *know* this by the sort of meditation Pascal takes us through is monumentally significant. Natural reason makes us lost, but in discovering its lostness, it also finds dignity and nobility in being aware of its situation.¹⁴

> All our dignity consists, then, in thought. It is from this that we must raise ourselves, and not from space and duration, which we could not fill. Let us labor, then, to think well. This is the principle of morality. (S232/L200)

What is it to think well? In large part it is to let reason delineate its limit, appreciate how lost we are, and thereby settle on the fact that we are

---

¹³ Gödel, Kurt (2003). *Collected Works: Volume IV: Selected Correspondence, A–G*. Edited by Solomon Feferman, John W. Dawson Jr., Warren Goldfarb, Charles Parsons, and Wilfried Sieg. Oxford: Clarendon Press: 427–439.

¹⁴ There are echoes of this thought in Camus' twentieth-century exploration of the absurd, *The Myth of Sisyphus*. There, Camus imagines a triumphant Sisyphus shaking his fists in defiance at the gods, though he remains far below them and stuck in the miserable and purposeless destiny they've assigned him.

1.3 Lost between Two Infinities

specks in the universe whose value is to comprehend this. As we will see in detail in later chapters, many people do not "think well" like this. Instead of thinking well, many people think of "dancing, playing the lute, singing, making verses, tilting at the ring, etc., about fighting, becoming king, without thinking of what it is to be king or to be man" (S513/L620). This feels pleasant in the moment, but it is disastrous, Pascal will argue.

Thinking well also requires using reason to conclude that we need an external anchor to make sense of ourselves and reality. That is to say that reason *does* play an important role in figuring things out, namely, the role of figuring out its limitations and its own insufficiency – this will look somewhat familiar to readers of Kant, but of course Pascal was writing long before Kant. The point is explicit in Pascal:

> Reason's final step is to recognize that there is an infinity of things beyond it. It is merely feeble if it does not go as far as realizing this. (S220/L188)

> There is nothing so consistent with reason as this denial [or disavowal] of reason. (S213/L182)

> All our reasoning reduces to giving in to feeling. (S455/L530)

Feeling is, as we have seen, the domain of the heart, which feels the heart-shaped void that the limits of reason draw.

It is worth considering, again, the currently pressing topic of artificial intelligence. The human being is frail and fragile in nature, as Pascal noted. Its basic inferential capacities are also dwarfed by those of machines (to which Pascal was no stranger – recall that he invented the first calculator). The machines need only some energy source to keep going; they can be made of metal and survive for eons. We are puny compared to what potentially could become a great technological, artificial civilization (if we can call it that) that dominates the world. But it would dominate it, it seems, only in the same sense that nature dominates our world: a hurricane can wipe out a city, a tsunami, as we've tragically seen, can kill hundreds of thousands. We are but fragile reeds, blowing this way or that according to the wind. But – and here I assume for illustration that we do not regard artificial intelligence as conscious or aware of things – we possess a nobility and dignity above all of this. Just as we comprehend our situation in nature, we can comprehend our situation in a world ruled by technology. We are not just machines, we are not just inferring this from that, in millions of steps per nanosecond like a computer. We are *aware* and we comprehend our situation. Our awareness constitutes our dominion over the physical world, whether it is populated by natural things or machines. We are capable of this awareness, first, because we are conscious, but just as importantly because our capacity to reason enables us to understand our situation. Both elements are necessary.

None of this is to say that machines cannot think, or reason. Another Pascalian insight that can help us understand the current state of technology is that reason, or "thinking," operates on an entirely different order than faith or the heart. It is sometimes asked aloud, "will AI replace us?" Even if AI can think and reason, and do so more or better than we can, the answer is still "no" for a Pascalian. We have something beyond reason: not only awareness of our situation (which some might argue machines can someday have as well) but also the heart. The heart is capable of affect, of will, and ultimately of faith. This puts us in an altogether different category of being than AI, at least according to the Pascalian picture. In later chapters we will see why this is a significant feature of the human.

Still, reason can do quite a lot. Most importantly, reason sees that it is not through reason that we can find our place. And furthermore, it sees that we cannot find our place anywhere within *ourselves*:

> Take comfort. It is not from yourself that you should expect it, rather, you should expect it by expecting nothing from yourself. (S234/L202)[15]

Here is where these reflections leaves us: that we cannot find within ourselves our place in the world and our significance, except to realize this, which is the only dignity for us. To find *comfort*, to find our true measure, we need an external anchor to measure ourselves against. We cannot expect it from ourselves.

> "What should I do? I see only darkness everywhere. Shall I believe that I am nothing? Shall I believe that I am God?" (S38/L3) [This is in

---

[15] This recalls John 15:5, "Apart from Me you can do nothing." (Thanks to Kevin McCain for pointing this out.)

quotation marks because it is part of an "order by dialogues" that Pascal meant in an interlocutor's voice. We will come back to this important fragment again below.]

What is it that is external to ourselves that can bring us comfort, significance, and explain what we are? As Pascal puts it in the midst of his mediation on the two infinities,

> [i]n the end, the greatest perceptible sign of God's omnipotence is that our imagination loses itself in this thought.

This may strike you as coming out of left field. What does God have to do with it, and how can our inability to make sense of reality be a sign of His power? This makes sense, I think, only once Pascal's full picture comes into view. One might naturally think here that Pascal's idea is that if God were anything but all powerful, we *could* understand him even as finite creatures that we are. In other words, we are limited, and so it is a sign of God's limitlessness that we cannot understand His creation (all of reality) or our place in it. But while this might be technically right on some standard theological views, I don't think this is what Pascal meant. Rather, as we will see in other contexts as well (e.g., when he considers why nature as we experience it does not prove that God exists), the imagination losing itself when trying to comprehend the world corroborates a particular conception of God, specifically the Christian one. It is the fact that we cannot make sense of ourselves without Him, but that we *can* figure out that this is the case, that is a sign of God's omnipotence, as it operates according to a particular theology, *the Fall*.

Skeptical limitations of our reason play a positive, essential role in the theology and apology of Pascal. We comprehend that there is a problem in need of a solution – that we are lost between the two infinities, that we cannot understand even how much we understand – but we cannot adequately comprehend what a solution would be:

> It is incomprehensible that God should exist, and incomprehensible that he should not; that the soul should be joined to the body, that we should have no soul, that the world should be created, that it should not, etc.; that original sin should be, that it should not. (S656/ L809)

Thus we cannot make sense, by reason, of the Christian picture, which, ultimately, Pascal will say is corroborated by our situation. We will return to this puzzling thought.

This section has focused on how the imagination loses itself between the two infinities, and it loses us along with it. What does this suggest about the imagination? In S643/L779 Pascal explains that it is often imagination that confuses and overtakes frail reason. The idea that the imagination is responsible for our cognitive overreach, that it pretends to provide reasons but mischievously only masquerades as reason, can be found throughout the early modern period. But as we have just noted, in Pascal this fact itself, that the imagination "loses itself," is taken to be a confirmation, somehow, of God's power.

There are several loose ends here. The most obvious for today's readers is why Pascal seems to ignore the many famous proofs of God's existence, and just assumes that reason cannot determine whether God exists. That is the subject of the next section.

1.4 Theological and Metaphysical Proofs

When considering how one might come to know a religious doctrine, such as that God exists and made the world with us in it, the contemporary student of philosophy probably thinks first of what Pascal regarded as "metaphysical" arguments: the argument from design, the cosmological argument, the ontological argument, and so on. And the student of theology might instead think first of the authority of the Church, the biblical testimony of miracles, and the like. People during Pascal's day would have had both in mind, but also the idea that one can see signs or evidence of God everywhere in creation. This third idea is less familiar today, but certainly would have been familiar to Pascal through various Biblical passages, classical sources such as Cicero, and later sources like Calvin and Montaigne.[16] However, Pascal rejected the idea that we can simply and convincingly *prove to a nonbeliever* that God exists, let alone the Christian doctrines, in any of these ways. To be sure, Pascal believed

---

[16] I explore this idea in detail in Avnur, Yuval (2024). Pascal's birds: Signs and significance in nature. *Philosophy and Phenomenological Research* 108 (1): 3–20.

1.4 Theological and Metaphysical Proofs

there were proofs of God and of Christianity. But whether these are effective methods of making anyone change their minds is a different matter. This rejection of evangelizing by appealing to proofs follows from Pascal's general skeptical outlook, in each case for a different reason.

Pascal's rejection of metaphysical arguments follows straightforwardly from his views about the place of reason in human life and purpose of religious faith.

> The metaphysical proofs of God are so remote from men's reasoning and so complicated that they make little impression. And when they are of service to some, it is only for the instant during which they see this demonstration. But an hour later they fear they have been mistaken. (S222/L190)

Reason itself, even if it is able to deduce some God, is unable to persuade most, and not for long. But what's more, Pascal rejects these proofs in principle. To begin with Scripture is the way to God for Pascal (S30/L411), and there are no such proofs found therein (S702/463). Moreover, the kind of God that might be metaphysically proved is not the God of the bible, not the God of Abraham with His specific history of interaction with humanity. Rather, it is the philosopher's God, a *deist* God which is abstract, an object with all perfections, but which has little to do with the human history, or the human condition and saving us from it. Pascal regarded such deist conceptions of God as equivalent to atheism (S690/L449), for reasons that will become clear when we consider divine hiddenness.

Finally, and most importantly, the result in the best-case scenario for these proofs is some sort of abstract knowledge. But this is, as Pascal saw it, useless for faith, by which he meant that it is useless for salvation and for redeeming humankind from its lost and corrupted nature. Instead, only *loving* God, and not on the basis of some abstract proof, can save us:

> What a distance there is between knowing God and loving him. (409/377)

Of course, loving God in some sense implicates God's existence, but Pascal rejected the idea that first you must prove the existence of the one you love, and only then can you love Him. The heart has its own kind of reasons, and they are *prior* to any proof or argument. Thus, at best a belief in God that is based on abstract reasoning is a distant second, and is itself insufficient:

> That is why those to whom God has given religion by intuition of the heart are very fortunate and, in fact, properly convinced. But [to] those who do not have it, we can give it only through reasoning, until God gives it to them by intuition of the heart. Without this, faith is only human and useless for salvation. (S142/L110)

We cannot, on our own without the grace of God, reason our way to the right kind of belief, the "intuition" of the heart. Pascal is trying not just to show the nonbeliever that God's existence follows from some premises, but that the resulting conviction deserves one's full, unrestrained and unqualified devotion. You have to feel something about the subject in order for the conclusion of the argument to matter. A metaphysical proof, on its own, can't make that happen. In an important fragment that we will examine in Chapters 2 and 3, S644/L781, we see even the argument from design – what many in his day (perhaps including himself) considered the most impressive proof of God's existence – merely gives nonbelievers reason to think the arguments of Christians are weak.

Pause for a moment to consider how radical a departure this is from the sort of debate we find in standard philosophy of religion today. Pascal's point is not to figure out what the best argument or proof is, reply to all objections, and thereby persuade the nonbeliever. Nor is it to defend the believer against atheistic arguments. All of this misses the point of Pascal's approach to religion. Without our hearts being in the right place, and without help from outside of us to move our hearts there, we are doomed. Instead of using reason to prove God, we should use reason to figure out that we are lost without God, that only God can help, and that we should open our hearts to that possibility. Rather than regarding the main subject matter of religion to be *proof* and *belief*, religion requires engagement from the whole human being. Belief will come later in the process. He even suggests, in S661/L820, that reason is not only limited in what it can show about the existence of God but also that it only produces weak proofs because it is "completely malleable." That is, it can seem to support almost anything we want it to. As we will see, for reason to lead us to the right place, we need to want the right things first, and what we want can determine what evidence is available to us in the first place.[17]

What about the theological proofs? This includes the testimony of others, especially about miracles and prophecies that came true. Pascal does not entirely disown these. But he certainly rejects them as a basis for establishing faith in the first place. The significance of these proofs is that they may show that one who already believes is reasonable – perhaps by lending faith a sort of consistency or evidential respectability. One with faith in one's heart takes on a whole system that includes, within it, some theological proofs, albeit ones such that you must already endorse the system in order to accept them. Perhaps for one with faith, such proofs can also facilitate reveling, awe, and even some details that are essential to faith. But, Pascal stresses, such theological proofs are not compelling to the nonbeliever, so they cannot themselves make the difference between a lost heathen and one of the faithful (S423/L835). They can only be appreciated from within.[18]

If this seems strange, question-begging, or circular, consider that one of the most popular responses to skepticism today is the so-called Moorean response. Moore "proved" that there is an external world like this: here is one hand, here is another (while waving his hands in front of himself).[19] Hands are external objects, so there is a world with external objects in it. Of course, many of us would reply that one who does not *already believe* that there are things like external objects/hands, that our senses do not massively deceive us, and so on, would never accept this proof. But why not accept it if you buy into the worldview of external objects and reliable senses? So, only those who already accept

---

[17] In S661/L821, Pascal attributes our deepest beliefs ("that tomorrow will dawn and that we shall die") to something he calls "custom." Again, we see echoes of this a generation later in Hume. In Pascal, though, this serves not only to show that reason itself is not the source of these deepest beliefs ("always to have proofs before us is too much trouble"), but that in order to have the deepest kind of belief, we must habituate ourselves, and make it the result of custom. This comes up, most famously, in the so-called wager, the topic of Chapter 5.
[18] This idea has had considerable influence. As elsewhere in his work, William James seems to take his cue from Pascal here in *The Variety of Religious Experience*, in which he suggests that such experiences may compel belief in the subject who undergoes the experience, but it need not compel beliefs in others. At the end of *I and Thou*, Martin Buber also remarks that though people who have had such experience may "bear witness" to these, they cannot serve as proof for others.
[19] Moore, George Edward (1939). Proof of an external world. *Proceedings of the British Academy* 25 (5): 273–300.

the conclusion, that there is an external world, are likely to buy the proof. Pascal, then, is saying something similar: someone who accepts religion may find some intense experience (or the testimony of a saint) to be clear indication that God operates in the world; but it doesn't follow that someone who does not already accept religion will take such an experience as any sort of indication. What makes Pascal so interesting is that he *himself* pointed this out, centuries before this issue became popular in analytic philosophy: such a "proof" can have no effect, and shouldn't, on someone who lacks faith.[20]

I may have lost you in that last paragraph. What could it mean to say that "from within" a system one appreciates "proofs" which cannot be appreciated from without? For the contemporary reader, this idea is potentially one of Pascal's most powerful, fascinating, and applicable today. It is a central idea for Pascal because it helps him to solve one of the biggest problems in theology, the apparent hiddenness of God.

One of Pascal's main preoccupations in the *Pensées* is the idea that God is hidden – "*Deus absconditus*" from Isaiah 45:15 appears several times. For someone without faith, the world does not look compellingly divine. While sometimes things in the world look nice and even inspiring, they never *look* like they are divinely inspired or Godly. This is simply a continuation of the skeptical theme: unless your heart is in just the right place, the theological arguments fall flat (much like Moore's proof falls flat for a skeptic or idealist), and metaphysical arguments underwhelm.

In more recent years, the atheist argument from divine hiddenness, admirably championed by John Schellenberg over many years and publications, has become one of the most widely discussed anti-religious arguments.[21] The argument is, very roughly, that if a relationship with God is highly valuable, then a good and powerful God would make such a relationship available to all who wanted it. But God does not make it available, he remains hidden for many even when they seek it. So, either the relationship is not so valuable or else a good and powerful God

---

[20] For an attempt to show how Moore (and so perhaps by association Pascal) could have been right while also explaining the dialectical ineffectiveness of the "proof," see Pryor, James (2004). What's wrong with Moore's argument? *Philosophical Issues* 14 (1): 349–378.

[21] See Schellenberg, John. (2015). *The Hiddenness Argument: Philosophy's New Challenge to Belief in God*. New York: Oxford University Press.

doesn't exist. Some Pascal scholars have thought that Pascal's take on this can be summed up by the title of Lezek Kolakowsi's classic book on Pascal: God owes us nothing! But I think matters are more subtle in Pascal.

According to Pascal's Augustinian version of the Fall, humans since leaving the garden of Eden are fallen. In their fallen state, they are closed off from God, they see and desire only the things of creation, or worldly things. We turned our backs on God, so He went away, not wanting to force us into a relationship. However, some of us somehow come to yearn for God again, and by grace He answers the call. Once He does, we can see clearly that creation has a creator, we feel clearly a love for this creator, and this love mediates our dealings with creation. We come to see the world (creation) clearly as the work of God, our beloved. So how the world, and life in it, looks depends on whether there is love in your heart – which is a kind of faith. This simple idea is summed up beautifully here:

> "Why, do you not yourself say that the sky and the birds prove God?" No. "And does not your religion say so?" No. For while this is true in a sense for some souls to whom God gave this illumination, nevertheless it is false for most of them. (S38/L3)

Whether the sky and birds – that is, the world as it simply appears to us – prove that God exists depends on whether you have already received God's grace. Elsewhere, in S644/L781, Pascal makes clear that he means those who already have faith, that the world appears to "prove" God "in a sense" in way distinct from any more complete or rigorous metaphysical proof such as the design argument. He also makes clear there that this difference, between those who see God in everything and those who don't, itself confirms the Christian religion's central doctrine of the Fall, because the Fall predicts that most, being turned away from God, won't see him, but those who are turned back toward God will live in his light. The hiddenness of God, for those who lack faith, is therefore not a valid objection against Pascal's version of Christianity, for the simple reason that this Christianity *predicts* that God will be hidden for them. Reason and experience, though they fail to prove God on their own, also fail to prove the absence of God. Pascal's skepticism about what reason and experience can say about the ultimate nature of things is absolute; it applies even to God's existence.

Despite all the limitations of our natural capacities, as presented in this chapter, it is important to emphasize that Pascal was no skeptic. He was harshly critical of Montaigne, who for Pascal represented the skeptic, for thinking that we lack true knowledge. Montaigne was right, Pascal thinks, to note that *reason* does not by itself produce knowledge, but he was wrong to stop there. In fact, his stopping at that, and advocating a sort of passive faith in place of knowledge, is seen by Pascal to be not only a tactical philosophical mistake but also a great moral failing (e.g., (S559/L680)).[22] Pascal's own positive view of knowledge and faith begins with what he calls "the heart."

Before turning to the heart, let us sum things up with the following fragment, which in a particularly poignant way weaves together several skeptical threads we've covered. Pascal is here imagining a person who realizes how lost they are but does not try to remedy it, and who fails to recognize the necessary role the heart can play if it is in the right place. Unlike this character, we must go on and try to find ourselves and our true situation:

> I do not know who put me into the world, nor what the world is, nor what I myself am. I am in terrible ignorance of everything. I do not know what my body is, nor my senses, nor my soul and even this part of me that thinks what I say, that reflects on everything and on itself, and knows itself no more than the rest. I see those terrifying spaces of the universe that surround me, and I find myself tied to one corner of this vast expanse, without knowing why I am put in this place rather than in another, nor why the short time given me to live is assigned to me at this point rather than at another of the whole eternity that preceded me or the one that will follow me.
>
> I see nothing but infinites on all sides, surrounding me like an atom and like a shadow that lasts only for an instant and returns no more.
>
> All I know is that I must soon die, but what I know least is this very death I cannot escape.
>
> As I do not know from where I come, so I do not know to where I am going, and I know only that, in leaving this world, I fall forever either

---

[22] This criticism of Montaigne plays out at length in *A Conversation with M. Sacy*. There, Pascal suggests that Montaigne failed to realize that, while skepticism correctly shows that our natural faculties cannot produce much knowledge, it also teaches us something positive about our natures (namely, that we are fallen but capable of greatness), and so he failed to realize that skepticism confirms the Fall.

1.4 Theological and Metaphysical Proofs

into nothingness or into the hands of an angry God, without knowing to which of these two conditions I must forever be allotted. Such is my state, full of weakness and uncertainty. (S681/L427)

Skepticism in philosophy, especially these days, is often reduced to an abstract puzzle about knowledge, or an intellectual curiosity, a paradox to try to solve. But for Pascal, skepticism leads to absolute existential terror, and the paradox we discover is not with our concept of knowledge, it is within ourselves. We cannot understand ourselves, we cannot understand life, without a workable solution. Pascal offers a classical but also a fresh perspective on a perennial philosophical problem. He brings skepticism home to the center of our very existence. The only way to address the problem is from our very center, the heart.

Whatever the heart does, we know at this point that it determines the basis of the operation of reason when it comes to geometry, and thinking about the world based on experience. It does this *naturally*, so that a normal human's heart will direct thought in more or less the same way (though we've seen that there is the possibility of some differences). But when it comes to supernatural or theological matters, humans are capable of two natures: one in which the heart reveals signs of God everywhere and produces faith, and another in which the heart does not. There is thus room for variability in the heart of a human in divine matters.

CHAPTER 2

The Heart

Pascal held that the state of your heart can determine not only what you love and want but also how you see things and what you believe. When he writes of the heart, Pascal often means what you are willing to accept and take for granted, which forms the background to your thinking. Commitment to one's family rather than one's boss, for example, might be the primary consideration in the background of one's decisions and thinking. That means, for Pascal, that one's heart favors and loves the family over the boss. The heart determines what we love, and love demands and provides reasons (for acting and for believing) that are otherwise irrelevant or unavailable. Though it may sound extreme to say that such love might even change the way the world looks, in this and the next chapter we will see that this is not only true to our phenomenology and ordinary experience, but that it is plausible even on reflection. Arguably, we actually do see things in a way affected by our hearts.

There is a difficulty, though, in discussing the heart in Pascal, because he appeals to the heart to play so many different roles in different contexts, and there is no sustained account of what the heart is in Pascal's work. At no point does he say "this is what I mean when I speak of the heart." Instead, we see that one and the same heart is responsible for natural knowledge of first geometrical principles, such as that any quantity can be multiplied, interpersonal love, decision-making or "the will," degrees of stubbornness, faith in God, and revelations of various kinds. It is hard to see how one and the same faculty can do all of these things. I will not attempt here a full defense of my reading of Pascal's "*Coeur*" (or heart). Rather, I will present an interpretation, or one thing the heart could be, and follow its consequences. Nothing I say, though, should be very controversial or shocking to the average Pascal scholar. However one understands the heart – a placeholder for different things, or one grand, essential, singular but unspecified element in Pascal – we will see that the way it is put to use by Pascal has profound relevance for us today.

2.1 Belief and the Heart

It may seem mysterious why a philosopher, and especially one who is also a mathematician, would associate the heart with belief at all. Shouldn't belief be about proof, evidence, and arguments? Tina Turner asked the right question: what's love got to do with it? The answer is that this particular philosopher/mathematician was steeped in and inspired by the Bible (and also Augustine), and the heart is found in the Bible to be connected to faith and belief in two key places. I say these are "key" because they are both famous and explicitly referenced by Pascal. Considering these influences will illuminate Pascal's usage.

The first and probably most obvious is the story of Pharoah in Exodus. It is written that God "hardened Pharoah's heart," causing him to stubbornly ignore the mounting evidence before him about the God of the Hebrews and His will. The hardening of the heart, then, is associated with an unwillingness to budge in one's course of action or belief, and to reject or refuse reasons otherwise. Pascal uses "hardening" in just this way most famously in S680/L423 (which is discussed later in this section).[1]

On the other hand, the heart can make you drawn to, rather than resistant to, some belief or faith. This is a softening of the heart, which Pascal explicitly cites from Psalm *119:36*, "Incline my heart,

---

[1] For those Pascal scholars who doubt that the heart in Pascal is related to this Biblical use, consider that the notion of hardening the heart is used, in just this way, in S260/L228, S580/L702, S693/L453, S728/L486, and S736/L496. Pascal also quotes Isaiah 63:17, which invokes the hardening of the heart in the same way. It is also worth noting that, in the Hebrew, the Pharaoh's heart in Exodus is not only hardened but also strengthened and made heavy. And, though much has been written about the fact that God hardens Pharaoh's heart, Pharaoh also hardens his own heart. So one can have some agency in this. See *The Hardened Heart* in Rabbi Jonathan Sacks, *Covenant and Conversation: A Weekly Reading of the Jewish Bible*. Maggid Books & the Orthodox Union, 2010.

O Lord, to your words, and not to selfish gain" in S412/L380 and S661/L821.[2]

In both cases, we can understand one's heart not only in terms of affective attraction or repulsion but also (perhaps consequently) the way that such attraction or repulsion is pursued. If you love dominance over, and the use of the labor of, the Hebrews, and your heart is hardened in this love, you will not only reject the demand of the God of the Hebrews to free them but you will also be stubborn when presented with evidence that this is what He demands, or that He even exists. You will obstinately hold to the existing arrangement in which the Hebrews are your slaves, come what may – you love your dominance faithfully, and your heart is hardened against anything that threatens it. In Pascal, if your heart one day is suddenly inclined toward the God of Christianity, it becomes easier for you to accept that the world is His creation. You will happily accept the glorious-looking sky as a sign of that God's glory, for example. The heart determines your will, not only in the sense of inspiring action on the basis of your love but also in the sense of what you are willing to consider seriously and what you are willing to dismiss as insignificant. As we've seen in the previous chapter, Pascal makes clear that our desires and our will determine a lot about how we see things and how we then go on to form beliefs:

> The will is one of the principal organs of belief, not that it creates belief, but because things are true or false according to the aspect from which we observe them. The will, which prefers one aspect to another, turns the mind away from considering the qualities of the one it does not care to see. And thus the mind, moving as one with the will, keeps looking at the aspect it likes, and so judges by what it sees. (S458/L436)

This can also be read as a development of an idea we found in *The Geometrical Mind*, in which we are drawn to the right conclusions in matters of faith by a force that "subdue[s] the rebellion of the will by an entirely celestial sweetness which charms it and transports it" (186). The heart attracts or repels, its polarity determines what it is drawn to or repulsed by, it generates desires that pull us toward or away from things, and this in turn changes the way we see things and the conclusions we

---

[2] He also cites inclining one's heart to God's words in Isaiah 41 in 735/489. A similar idea is found in Romans (ii.14–15), in which a law is "written in the hearts" of gentiles.

reach. In a sense, the heart thus generates a feel for things, one might call it an "intuition," since it brings things to our attention that would not have been attended to otherwise. Our heart feels in the sense of its being affective, but it also feels *something*, that which our love leads us to focus on. (Some commentators have called this "intuition," though this brings to mind Cartesian intuition, which I doubt Pascal meant to evoke here.)

As mentioned in the previous chapter, since the feeling of the heart, as a result of the will it generates, affects the formation of belief, the account sounds like what contemporary psychologists call "motivated reasoning." We tend to reason in a way that resonates with our desires and fears. But on Pascal's view, this is not a mere pathology or the mark of a weak and irrational mind. *All* reasoning is motivated reasoning. There is no other way to look at the world but under the influence of *some* will. There is no blank default, there is no heartless view, because in order to look, you have to be a person with a heart looking. We are not, and cannot become, heartless machines processing data. We are fundamentally beings that are drawn to and repelled by various things, and only consequently are we believers. However you see things, this is influenced by the state of your heart, because your heart is always *somewhere*, you always love *something* (even if only yourself). In the words of Bob Dylan, you have to serve *somebody* (even if it's always yourself). And Pascal held this completely generally, and held to it systematically. As we've seen, not even basic principles of geometry can be determined by reason alone, we accept it only due to the natural state of our hearts. The heart gets us going in all cases, in every way, on all matters of thinking and acting.

And yet the heart's state can be affected by things external to you. How your thinking will go, and even how you see the world is determined by whatever decides your heart. In the case of geometry, nature determines the relevant aspect of your heart. But consider other cases. Your daughter, for example, may affect you deeply, in a way and with a force that you cannot summon on your own. Since you love your daughter – which is to say you are in a particular relation to her – you will hear her a certain way at her singing recital. You're motivated to think she is an extraordinary singer, and this might lead you to miss how well some other children sang. That is classic motivated reasoning, perhaps even motivated perceiving. Your daughter and your affection for her – not just your sensory and reasoning faculties – determine what you perceived and what you missed in the recital.³

But here Pascal would point out that it might go just the other way: you love your daughter, but also love your own objectivity and reason, perhaps your heart is vain, and you like to display (to yourself and others) how objective and neutral you are. And so you downplay the quality of your daughter's performance, you refuse to perceive it, your vanity hardens your heart. Here too you are motivated, but by your vanity or perhaps your repulsion to partiality. You might actually miss or downplay some comparatively good qualities in her voice, in this case. As Pascal puts it, we can become "most unjust as counterbalance" (L78/S44).

This provides an important insight for us today. We all agree that wishful thinking (to put the idea of motivated reasoning in its most basic form) is irrational. The irrationality is bad from the perspective of accuracy, or our aim to believe true things (and avoid believing false things). From this perspective, it is bad to think, for example, that climate change is fake only because you like the presidential candidate who is against regulating polluting industries. It's bad to handle the relevant evidence on the basis of the desire to fit in with the people of one political party rather than another. That might seem to suggest that, if only you didn't have that desire, you might reason more rationally. You should strive to be an unbiased, dispassionate thinker.

But is there really a clean, sterile, non-motivated way to reason, like a machine? Yes, we want to say. And when we say that, we think of how a mathematician reasons, as the prime example of dispassionate, neutral reasoning. But Pascal, no stranger to mathematics, points out that even mathematicians have to start somewhere before they prove things – the heart provides the first principles – and, of course, a mathematician

---

[3] There is empirical evidence for, and plenty of philosophical discussion of, the phenomenon of our affective states affecting what we perceive. One version of this is what Susanna Siegel calls "wishful seeing," in Siegel, Susanna (2017). How is wishful seeing like wishful thinking? *Philosophy and Phenomenological Research* 95 (2): 408–435. For discussion of related empirical work, see Balcetis, Emily & Dunning, David (2006). See what you want to see: Motivational influences on visual perception. *Journal of Personality and Social Psychology* 91 (4): 612–625, and Molden, Daniel. & Higgins, Edward (2012). Motivated reasoning. In Keith Holyoak and Robert Morrison (eds.), *Oxford Handbook of Thinking and Reasoning*.

2.1 Belief and the Heart

might be motivated by the desire to prove herself right, to prove a rival mathematician wrong, and so on. In fact, Pascal would criticize the ambitious mathematician on the basis that vanity, the lust for glory, propels her inquiry. Human reasoning never happens in a motivational vacuum.[4]

The next natural question is whether all motivations, states of the heart, are equally good, or whether some are preferable. Pascal's answer is clear: some states of the heart are better than others. We might never be "neutral," but we can be objective in the sense that the objectively correct aspect of reality motivates us. That is not to say *merely* that it is always right to love the truth or neutrality, for example, since we've seen that this can warp and blind us too. Rather, what is right is that we love that which is actually, objectively worthy of love, or lovable. But that doesn't mean that the best, most correct way to generate your beliefs is not motivated, or that it is based on reason all the way down; it's still motivated. Reality is a certain way, and this makes some things *worthy* of *correct* love and attraction. The universe is not just a mechanism; some things are objectively lovable. The best starting point in inquiry and belief, or the best way for your heart to be, is to be aligned with what is worthy of love given the way reality actually is. The way to align with what is worthy of love is, of course, just to love it.

Moreover, Pascal held that loving the wrong thing (the subject of Chapter 4) leads to misery, not just to bad believing. There is also a practical reason to love the right thing. This also gives you a hint about what the right thing to love is: how does your life go when you love it? But, focusing for now on beliefs, the fact that some states of the heart are better aligned with reality than others does *not* mean that some people are operating with reason all the way down, that the correct and rational people do not have the heart, rather than reason, at the foundation of their worldview.

This is captured by one of the most famous fragments of the *Pensées*:

> The heart has its reasons, which reason does not know. We know this in a thousand things. I say that the heart loves the universal being naturally and itself naturally, according to its practice. And it hardens itself against

---

[4] To say that no reasoning is unmotivated is not to say all motivated reasoning is equal. Some reasoning might be more motivated, and motivated by a more warping desire, than another.

one or the other as it chooses. You have rejected the one and kept the other. Is it through reason that you love yourself? (S680/L423)

The first sentence states clearly that the heart has its own reasons outside of, and as we have seen prior to, the faculty of reason. If one state of the heart is better than the other, it is not because it is better supported by reason. Pascal then goes on to give an important example: reason is not the source of our self-love, the prime motivator according to most standard theories of human nature and motivation. You love yourself, you are motivated to pursue your self-interest, *not* because you've reasoned to that conclusion. Rather, you do so "naturally" as a fallen human. We will see soon that this part of your nature can change, but first we will need to see about natural aspects of the heart that all humans share, which cannot change.

2.2 Geometry and the External World as Matters of the Heart

We have seen that the heart can affect what one believes, because the heart is the seat of affect, and affect can steer the belief-forming process. But there is much more to the heart in Pascal. In Chapter 1, we saw Pascal attributing belief in first principles and basic concepts, as well as our conviction that this is not one long dream, to the heart. How do we understand such things as a matter of affect?

There are two important aspects of the heart that make sense of how it is involved in geometry and the external world. The first is that the heart determines, by how hardened or inclined it is, how easy or difficult it is for someone to believe something. It determines, for example, how certain you feel and how willing you are to budge, as in Pharoah's case. The second is that Pascal repeatedly calls our certainty in first principles *natural*, from the earlier essays through to the *Pensées*. Something about human natures makes our hearts accept certain first principles and reject skepticism, but human nature is compatible with different stances on how significant we regard our lives and whether there is a God. When it comes to those latter things, different people go different ways, and Pascal took on the task of addressing and convincing the wrong-hearted people to change. Armed with these two points, we can understand the application of the heart to geometry and the external world.

2.2 Geometry and the External World

Begin with geometry. Recall what Pascal wrote in S142/L110:

> For knowledge of first principles, such as space, time, motion, number, [is] as firm as any we derive from reasoning, Reason must use this knowledge from the heart and instinct, and base all its arguments on it. The heart feels that there are three dimensions in space and numbers are infinite, and reason then shows that there are no two square numbers of which one is double the other. Principles are felt, propositions are proved; all with certainty, though in different ways. And it is as useless and absurd for reason to demand from the heart proofs of its first principles before accepting them, as it would be for the heart to demand from reason an intuition of all demonstrated propositions before receiving them. (S142/L110)

The heart feels (*sent*) principles (here and again in S680/L424) and knows things firsthand (*connaissons*) (e.g., S142/L11). Recall that Pascal regards the universal (or near universal) acceptance of the basics of geometry as natural knowledge. A simple way to understand this is that our hearts are naturally completely hardened to the basics (space, number, etc.). Reason might confuse some of us, but we are ultimately wedded by nature to such claims as every number has a successor, that there are three dimensions in space, and so on. That is to say, even more than Pharoah, we will not budge given our natures, and much else follows from this. When presented with an object, for example, we might want or reject it. Either way, the object is presented to us in space and time. However the will deals with this object, it deals with it spatially and temporally. Our will, generated by the heart, is fundamental, and it follows from our will that we feel space with its various Euclidean characteristics. Geometry thus deals with how our hearts operate – they operate spatiotemporally – and this is so fundamental to our natures that we are entirely unable to consider things, as objects of our wills, otherwise. When we think of an *intuition* that, say, two parallel lines never meet, we are *seeing* something in the way we automatically relate to things.[5]

Turn now to the long dream from Chapter 1. How do you know that life is not like a long dream, with your nightly dreams grafted on to it?

---

[5] This proto-Kantian idea that, in Pascal, first principles can be analyzed in this way by every possible condition of the heart is suggested by Moriarty (ibid.).

How do you know that you are currently in contact with reality, rather than phantasms? Again, Pascal's answer was that this is a matter of the heart, that we are naturally incapable of taking this life to be anything but real. This was contrasted with Descartes' answer, which depended on reason (a proof that there is a non-deceiving God). What Pascal means in rejecting the Cartesian picture is that our hearts are naturally hardened against the possibility that this is all a long dream. Again, one can take this to be an implication of the way we love: we love things in this world with such seriousness and devotion (for some of us, the thing we love this way is ourselves, what we regard as the real and waking self) that it simply follows that those things are regarded, in loving them so, as real. So our hearts, in their devotion to things in this "life," are thereby hardened to be incapable of seriously considering that this all – including our beloved – is a long dream. You can pretend it isn't real, and may even deceive yourself. But the typical human, at least, naturally cannot take it seriously. Skepticism is like kissing someone you don't really like: your heart is not in it and you're not being true to yourself. Thus, it is not *reason* that provides this foundation, but the heart.

Rather than taking what Hume called, derisively, an "unexpected circuit" to prove that there is a non-deceiving God as Descartes did, Pascal appealed to the heart as the foundation of these beliefs. In part, this is because Pascal, like many of us today, rejected metaphysical "proofs," such as those that Descartes appealed to. Specifically, he rejected them because *our hearts are not in it* when it comes to such proofs. To Pascal it seemed silly to try to prove something that your heart already committed you to. This is what makes Pascal's epistemology *cordate*, rather than empiricist or rationalist.

Perhaps we are victims of Descartes' deceiving demon, so what we naturally feel certain about is not true. Maybe this is one long dream. I am incapable of taking those possibilities seriously, but they are possibilities. This shows that it is out of our hands, beyond the reach of reason, to confirm our certainties, and that instead our certainty is a matter of the heart. The question is whether our hearts are aligned in the right way, and whether we love the right things. How this can be a matter that is beyond reason, and what this means for whether we are rational, are good questions. It will help, in addressing them, to consider cases in which human hearts can diverge. Some feel that this life is epically significant, others think it is ultimately frivolous. Some have faith in their hearts, others see nothing but Descartes' mechanistic universe (minus his God who is standing around watching). We now turn to Pascal's main point, and main philosophical use of the cordate epistemology: disagreement in faith, revelation, and divine hiddenness.

2.3 Divine Hiddenness in the Light of the Heart

We have just seen that the heart reveals first principles about space by providing unshakable feelings about it. Just as our hearts reveal principles about space, they also can reveal more specific things about the world, and thereby make such things available to reason. What things these are depends on what we love, and of course on what the world has to offer.

In the *Pensées*, Pascal is trying to address the nonbeliever, the one without faith or a love of God in the heart. To do this, Pascal makes every effort to get into the mind and heart of the nonbeliever. In later chapters we will see that Pascal thought that much else is wrong with the nonbeliever besides lacking the right *belief*. Here we are going to confine ourselves only to the lack of belief. The nonbeliever looks around at the world, and though they might see something beautiful or even inspiring, they don't take any of it to be a sign of anything divine. In contrast, the true believer sees God's work everywhere in the world, so that God seems *obvious* to them. The difference is in the heart: the believer loves God (more than themselves), and in virtue of this much is revealed in their experience:

> wanting to appear without disguise to those who sought him with their heart, and hidden from those who flee from him with all their heart, he has modified our recognition of him, giving visible signs to those who seek him and none to those who do not. (S182/L149)

It is the heart that determines whether you seek or flee God – whether you are hardened against him like Pharoah, who consequently refused all signs of God. The secular reader may balk at this: "I don't believe in the sort of magic involved in 'giving visible signs' to those who believe." Though it takes some familiarity with the Augustinian theology of the

Fall, understanding Pascal's view here does not require any belief in signs magically appearing, or even anything supernatural at all. As we will see, in general, it is possible to understand Pascal's point here even for the nonbeliever because Pascal held that the world is ambiguous (see Chapter 3), it contains no compelling signs or mechanisms to make the atheist believe.

We have seen that reason and experience themselves don't tell us much about the world, not even whether this is all a long dream, let alone whether God made the world. Pascal was fond of quoting Isaiah 45:15 "*Vere tu es Deus Absconditus.*" He references it four different times in the *Pensées* and alludes to it in some of his longest and most powerful fragments. It means, "Truly you are a hidden God." We might instead put it more neutrally like this: if there is a God, He is hidden. For Pascal, this can be said without embarrassment, by both the believer and nonbeliever; on this they agree! And yet it is a substantial constraint on any theological view that it must conform to it. He held a theology according to which God does not make himself unambiguously present, for all to see in the world, and in fact thinks that this is the only viable kind of theology. To see the truth requires more than simply looking around, so the fact that you have looked and assessed, and found no God, is not yet a good indication that there is no God, according to this theology. We must consider, then, why Pascal thought that seeing the truth requires more than simply looking around.

One reason is that God is not literally to be seen – not exactly. In the most straightforward sense, that we don't *literally* see God should be relatively uncontroversial to any non-Pagan and non-pantheist. If God is not literally here among us, then why would you expect to see Him when you look around? Even if you experience things *as* Godly or divine, this is not to say that you directly see God. God is not literally identical to the world, to nature, to the sun, or anything like that. At least not for Pascal, who following Augustine strongly distinguished himself from pantheists and pagans.

This is not to say, though, that no one has direct contact. In the Hebrew Bible a few people are said to directly perceive God, Moses most directly. Moreover, some claim to have mystical experiences which purport to directly contact God even today. Pascal had such a mystical experience, which he described in "The Memorial," a short, ecstatic

2.3 Divine Hiddenness in the Light of the Heart

poem he had sown into his jacket. So when Pascal says God is hidden, he does not mean either that we do not literally see God in the world or that it is impossible to have mystical experiences of God.

Rather, what Pascal meant by God's hiddenness, the notion that you cannot discover God by looking around, is that it is possible (and even common) to experience the world without any indication of God. That is, it is possible never to see things *as* Godly. What is it to see things as Godly? David perhaps never had direct contact with God like Moses did. Instead, David saw *God's glory* in the sky (Psalm 19), rather than God Himself. And others throughout history saw *the work* of God in miracles and in nature. For them, God is no longer hidden. But for many of us, God remains hidden, because although the sky might look glorious, it doesn't seem to us to declare God's glory.[6]

If God makes the earth go round, and you know this, then watching the progress of the sun across the sky amounts to knowingly witnessing God's work. But if you don't believe that God makes the earth go round, then you can watch the sun's progress without recognizing any indication that it is God's work. This generalizes to all things in nature. It isn't obvious that this world was created by the God of Abraham, at least not to everyone. At the same time, it isn't obvious that the world was *not* created by a god. Even the atheist has to admit that the sky can look glorious, and so *potentially* or *possibly* in being glorious it could be the declaration of a creator's glory. The world is thus ambiguous in our collective experience. But, if there is a God, and if it is important and good for us to know Him, shouldn't it at least be obvious to us that He exists, so we can make an informed choice whether to be devoted to Him? This is how Pascal frames the problem:

> This is what I see and what troubles me. I look in all directions and see only darkness everywhere. Nature offers me nothing that is not a matter of doubt and concern. If I saw nothing in it that revealed a divinity, I would come to a negative conclusion, if I saw everywhere the signs of a creator, I would settle down peacefully in faith. But, seeing too much to deny and too little to reassure me, I am in a pitiful state, in which I have

---

[6] There is admittedly an ambiguity in the notion of experiencing God here. Here I am discussing *visible signs* as in the Pascal quote. That for many people there is an absence of visible signs is consistent with the notion that Christians can experience God in other ways too (through the Holy Spirit, for example).

wished a hundred times that if a God maintains nature, it should proclaim him unequivocally, and that if the signs it gives are deceptive, it should suppress them altogether, nature should say all or nothing, that I might see which side I ought to take. Instead, in my present state, not knowing what I am and what I must do, I know neither my condition nor my duty. My whole heart longs to know where the true good is in order to follow it. Nothing would be too costly for eternity. I envy those of the faith whom I see living with such unconcern and who make such a poor use of a gift that, it seems to me, I would use so differently. (S682/L429)

Some believers will recoil at this idea. "Nonsense!" they say, "I see God everywhere and everything in life proves God!" It is one of Pascal's great insights that this person is not exactly disagreeing with the previous paragraph. It is possible for some to see signs of God everywhere, and it is possible for others not to see any signs at all. This is a difference in their hearts which alters the way each sees the world. We come again to this vivid fragment:

'So, do you not say, yourself, that the sky and the birds prove God?' No. 'And does your religion not say so?' No. For while that is true in a sense for some souls to whom God gave this enlightenment, it is nevertheless false in respect of the majority. (S38/L3)

In the context of the idea that our senses fail to show us, on their own, that God exists, we can take this as a significant indication that although *the senses themselves* don't reveal God, God can be revealed through the senses to those with faith in their hearts. This is in just the same way that although the senses don't reveal that this experience of a table is not part of a long dream, we know it is a real table and not part of a long dream because of our hearts. To those who are unbelievers (or rather non-lovers), this sounds laughably inadequate. The sky looks nice, glorious even. But there's nothing Godly there. What makes Pascal so unique is that, rather than reject this secular reaction by insisting it is wrong, or that it is based on a misapprehension of the world, he accepts that the world can look Godless. He does this by *explaining* it, subsuming it under his theological picture. This philosophical Judo is a fascinating maneuver to be admired for its logic alone. The Pascalian *predicts* that the sky would look Godless to one without the love of God in one's heart. So the sky's looking Godless cannot itself be evidence against Christianity.

The difference between the heart making it certain that this isn't a long dream and the heart making it appear that God made the world is a difference in *human nature*. All humans – or almost all, as noted, it is possible that in some circumstances one avoids this – have hearts that are disposed to regard the objects of the senses as *real*. I have suggested one way to understand this: the heart loves *as real* many things in the world, so it is impossible to regard those things as unreal with any seriousness. But not *all* humans have hearts that are disposed to see God's work in nature. In fact, typical humans since biblical times are disposed in the opposite direction. This follows from Pascal's Augustinian theology of the Fall – that we are in a fallen state in which our hearts are in the wrong place – and this affects the way we see the world. Those who love God see the world as His creation, and those who don't love God see only the things in the world as objects, not as creations. So for those with love in their hearts, the world is full of signs, but for others there are no signs (see Chapter 3 for more on how this works).

The world can be experienced as God's world, or as a Godless, heartless mechanism.[7] According to what we might call (on Pascal's behalf) a naïve philosopher's theology, this is a good argument against God's existence. If God were a perfectly good and loving creator and found it valuable for us to have a relationship with Him, then He would make Himself apparent so that we all can have that relationship. But He clearly doesn't do *that*. So such a God doesn't exist. However, this is not Pascal's theology. According to Pascal's Augustinian theology of the Fall, God gives enough indication for those that want to believe, but is hidden enough so that those who don't want to believe are not compelled by the evidence. The world is, in other words, *strategically* ambiguous. This is not the God of the philosophers, which Pascal calls a "false God" (S690/L449). It is, as Pascal sometimes puts it, an angry God who has been forsaken, one with a specific history in dealings

---

[7] I borrow this phrase from Malcolm, Norman (1992). The groundlessness of belief. In R. Douglas Geivett, & Brendan Sweetman (eds.), *Contemporary Perspectives on Religious Epistemology*. New York: Oxford University Press. Chapter 6.

with us as told by the Bible, through Augustinian interpretation, and one whose decisions and justice (as we will see) we cannot possibly comprehend.

This renunciation of the God of philosophers by one of the great religious philosophers is itself a reason to read Pascal today, because the God of the philosophers has been so dominant. His rejection of this abstract God and embrace of the God of Abraham (the God of the Bible) is also significant when comparing him to Descartes. In fact, he seemed angry with Descartes for pushing the idea that God is an abstract entity, perfect and crystalline orbiting outside of all of creation, ready for us to simply deduce him and then all is well. Pascal "could not forgive" Descartes for giving God no place in human life, and in the world, except to give it an initial nudge.[8] But today most of philosophy of religion, and most of the arguments of the new atheists, concern one of two Gods: the crystalline philosopher's or Deist God, or a personal God which is taken to be literally described in the bible, as if he is being mapped out descriptively throughout. Pascal shows how to think about religion, and religious belief, without taking it either way: the philosopher's God is a false God, but to think that the Bible literally describes God is to conflate two different orders of reality: the physical and the spiritual; and two different methods: reason and the heart. Scripture can be understood as a guide to loving God, not describing Him or the physical world.

To appreciate how drastically different Pascal's God is from the God we are used to in standard debates today, we will have to briefly examine this theology. This will also clarify the difference between belief that this is not a long dream and belief in God.

2.4 The Fall: A Tale of Two Hearts

According to Pascal's Augustinian theology of the Fall, your "second nature" – that is, your nature as a human born after the Fall – determines that you are by default inclined toward yourself and worldly

---

[8] This is from a fragment attributed to Pascal, but not authenticated, known as Lafuma 1001 and Brunschwig 77: "I cannot forgive Descartes. In all his philosophy he would have been quite willing to dispense with God. But he had to make Him give a fillip to set the world in motion; beyond this, he has no further need of God."

2.4 The Fall Tale of Two Hearts

things, rather than the creator of those things. This is determined by events external to you, over which you have no power, including the expulsion from Eden. So again, as is the case with geometrical first principles and the external world, events and beings external to you determine your heart and your fundamental orientation toward the world. You did nothing to make your nature such that your heart feels the first principles that it does, you're just born with a will that deals with spatial things and feels things accordingly.

Loving yourself means, essentially, grasping at things *within* creation to serve yourself, another part of creation. You may love things in the world, such as your family members, but it is in virtue of their relation to you, your history with them for example, that your heart is moved. Pascal calls this "concupiscence," though he means more than just lust. The heart is in this way cut off from God, the creator. Concupiscence is creation uselessly playing with itself, ignoring the creator.[9]

The faithful who love God instead of themselves do so only by God's grace. God in that case inclines the heart, softens it so that you are not so resistant to belief, and you are then drawn to the form of life that is best suited to you and most true: a faithful lover of God living in His creation; you are then saved. Though I have not emphasized this nearly as much as Pascal would have, this happy situation would require an intermediary, Jesus Christ, because the world otherwise has already been cut off from God. For Pascal, this means that your heart falls in love with that which is beyond the worldly things, that which created them and you. This is to love that which is ultimately *worthy* of being loved, so it is to love correctly, for only by loving God can you see and understand God's creation and your place in it.

This raises a number of questions, which we must briefly address. How does God decide whose heart to incline, by Grace, or whom to save? This was a matter of great controversy among Christians for a long time, including during Pascal's life. Arguably it was *the* main question that he and his associates took programmatic and public positions on. Key to this controversy is whether humans have it within their own power to be saved, or whether it is completely out of their hands and up

---

[9] The notion of creation "playing with itself" is due to Harry Frankfurt, who made this remark while discussing Spinoza at a seminar I attended some twenty years ago.

to God's dispensation of grace. Is your eternal fate predetermined, or based on the free decisions you make? Though this is a fascinating question, and though Pascal (as a so-called "Jansenist") had a position on it, we won't get into detail about it in this book. What we can see so far is that, for Pascal, if you truly and genuinely *seek* – which meant for him that you *want* to love God more than yourself – then God will grant you the grace necessary. But truly and genuinely seeking is not so straightforward. How do you get yourself to really, genuinely *want* something that you don't currently want? And is there a *guarantee* that God will answer your call when you truly seek? We will take this up later in Chapter 5.

Pascal did not believe that seeking God was a matter of seeking an item in nature, like looking for the holy grail or trying to find a halo around the head of a guru. In fact, it is not seeking in any physical or visual sense, like a detective seeks a clue. Rather, to seek is to want to see things a certain way by feeling a certain way. Once you "find" God, there are signs everywhere. It is like seeking the world as you've never seen it, seeking that which is behind the world. Nor is seeking a matter of going around looking for arguments, either empirical ("look, the beauty of this sky proves God!") or metaphysical ("look, the orbits of the planets are so perfect, they must have been designed by a God!"). This is how he puts it:

> This is what Scripture indicates to us, when it says in so many places that those who seek God will find him. That light is not spoken of like the midday sun. We do not say that those who seek the midday sun, or water in the sea, will find it. And hence the evidence of God must not be of this kind in nature. So it tells us elsewhere: Truly, you are a God who hides himself. (S644/L781)

To seek God is, essentially, to seek to love something that you do not yet love. You are looking for love, but you do not have it within yourself to simply become inspired to love something. Something, a potential beloved, has to charm you, affect you in the right way. And, even more difficult, in this case seeking means to want to love something *instead* of what you already love. It means to try to love something more than you love yourself, to want something that you do not want, when you want something else even more. But like Bonnie Raitt sang, you can't make your heart feel something it won't. This is an impossible task to accomplish on one's own. For this kind of change of heart you need help, supernatural help from the order of divinity, from God.

We have just covered, very briefly and in bare outline, a lot of theology. It is necessary to do this in order to understand how the heart works in Pascal, and why. But if you are familiar with contemporary discussions of divine hiddenness (and the problem of evil), you might think that all of this is implausible and perhaps incoherent. It just doesn't make sense why God, who wants us to love him, makes it so hard to even see that he exists, let alone to love him. Why withhold from us until You feel like granting us grace? Why am I born with this bad heart, when it was not I but Adam and Eve who betrayed God? The notion of inherited sin that the Fall is based on seems to make very little moral sense to us. So far we have been focusing on the consequence of concupiscence, our second nature since the Fall, for how we see things and what we believe. But it gets worse than that, as we will see in a later chapter: it makes us miserable, and we are thoroughly corrupted by it. But this just makes the question more pressing: why would God punish us with this concupiscent nature, and withhold our salvation unless we pursue something that it is impossible for us to see in this state that he put us in, and all because of a grudge against a distant ancestor with whom we have almost no connection?

Pascal was sensitive to this reaction, and in fact in a sense he agrees: it makes no sense. But that is just to say that it is beyond the limits of reason, and Pascal would have predicted it so, since as we have seen he held that the order of divine things is beyond the reach of reason. Here is how he puts his answer:

> It is, however, astonishing that the mystery most distant from our knowledge, that of the transmission of sin, should be a thing without which we can have no knowledge of ourselves.
>
> For without doubt there is nothing more shocking to our reason than to say that the sin of the first man has made culpable those who, being so remote from this source, seem incapable of participating in it. This transmission not only seems impossible to us, it even appears very unjust. For what is more contrary to the rules of our wretched justice than the eternal damnation of a child, incapable of will, for a sin in which he seems to have so little part that was committed six thousand years before

him? Certainly nothing shocks us more harshly than this doctrine. And yet without this most incomprehensible of all mysteries, we are incomprehensible to ourselves. The knot of our condition takes its twists and turns in this abyss, so that man is more unintelligible without this mystery than this mystery is unintelligible to man.

Thus it seems that God, wanting to reserve for himself alone the right to teach us about ourselves and to render the difficulty of our existence unintelligible to ourselves, has concealed the knot so high – or rather we should say so low – that we were quite incapable of reaching it. As a result, it is not through the proud exertions of our reason, but through its simple submission, that we can truly know ourselves. (S164/L131)

To the contemporary reader, especially one familiar with the standard criticisms of religion today, this may sound like just a bunch of hand waving. Isn't Pascal simply saying that we cannot make sense of it but it's true anyway and you had better believe it? Why should we accept this? Today's readers, who are likely to also be aware of past occasions in which we have renounced a previous generation's values, should first consider that our inability to comprehend the justice in inherited sin might be due to our inability to grasp justice accurately in general. After all, humans have collectively changed their minds about what justice demands throughout history, so humility about our current convictions seems reasonable. Pascal also suggests this, explaining that we cannot judge God "by the rules of our wretched justice," because we ourselves are poor judges of justice (S94/L60).

But perhaps more importantly for the purpose of this book, what Pascal is saying here is perfectly consistent with his general framework: we moderns have put too much stock in reason, and our situation should not be expected to make sense to us through the operation of our reasoning faculties. Human nature is corrupt and paradoxical, not a puzzle that can be resolved logically. In fact, *this is what the very view in question, the Fall, predicts*: in our current, post-fall state, we will be confused, deformed, corrupt, and unable to make sense of the world or ourselves, but we will be so vain and arrogant as to think that whatever is true and important can be figured out by our own little faculty of reason. So the fact that the Fall, the story of our nature, fails to make sense to us is just another box to check confirming the view. Or, at least, that it fails to make sense shouldn't count as a refutation of that view, since its failure to make sense is predicted by it.

Let's take stock of where we are. The problem of divine hiddenness is really a problem of ambiguity in the world (or in nature): for the nonbeliever, there are no clear signs in the world that God exists, that this or that religion is true. According to Pascal's religious idea, an Augustinian theology of the Fall, the hearts of humans since the fall are typically corrupted by concupiscence – they love themselves and the world rather than God – and only by God's grace can a person's heart be changed from this. This addresses the problem of ambiguity in more than one way. As we saw in the beginning of this chapter, the state of your heart can affect how you see things, so God is hidden to some and apparent to others, depending on their hearts. Furthermore, there is a religion which predicts that the world is ambiguous in the way that we find it to be, and that is Christianity according to the Fall. Rather than an objection to Christianity, then, the problem of hiddenness is an objection to all of Christianity's rivals, which do not predict that their God or gods are hidden, visible only to some. In the rest of this chapter, we will see how Pascal works out these ideas. In particular, we will look at how it might be that one's heart determines how one sees things, and how it could be that divine ambiguity actually confirms Christianity. In the next chapter we will consider what this would mean for us today.

2.5 The Heart's Own Reasons

Recall Pascal's famous statement that the heart has its own reasons, and that it is not reason that determines that you love yourself (concupiscence) rather than God (faith) (S680/L423). The heart has its own reasons in two ways, potentially: reasons to love, and the reasons that love generates. What reason is there ever to love something? This is, the rest of his famous quote makes clear, not a matter of reason. It is a matter of "sweetness" (as in the "celestial sweetness" with which one can be "charmed" (186)). What reasons does the heart generate? They are the reasons generated by the aim of pursuing the object of your love or commitment. Your commitment to your family, for example, gives you reason to dwell on some things (a potential insurance policy) rather than others (a potential solo vacation). That much is straightforward, as clear and plausible as that no exercise of reason is required for such a commitment to family (such as it is). Rather, one does it out of love (or obligation, or shame) or perhaps as a default orientation in life. To reason about it seems like one thought too many. As Pascal directly states, you didn't reason your way to loving yourself. Even if you did, that would be superfluous and weak (like the metaphysical proofs of God are). This is a matter of the heart, not reason.

But beyond these points, it seems Pascal noticed something further that the heart generates: it can give experience an added significance. Recall that for those with faith in their hearts, the sky and the birds prove God, at least "in a sense" (S38/L3). Perhaps this is because the sky and birds take on a different significance, and even *look* different, or are grasped differently, by those who love the creator of the sky and birds. To such a person, everything in the world is a sign of God and everything has the added significance of having been made by one's beloved:

> for it is certain [that those] with living faith in their hearts see at once that all existence is nothing other than the work of the God they adore. (S644/L781)

This can explain not only why things look different to those who love God than they do to those who don't but also that to understand the world, to see it right, you need to first love God.

The notion that what you love can change how you see things is not restricted to religious matters. Consider first how the significance of objects in general depends on your relation to people. I very much love my daughter and often miss her while she's away at school. Imagine that I go to pick her up, and as I wait at the front of the school for her class to be over, I notice a display of paintings that all the children have made that day. Naturally, I skip over most of them until I find my child's. I pause and look at it intently, adoring it and all its features. How lovely! Her cute little fingers painted a sky and some birds, she must have been feeling happy today. Details pop out, associations with other things I know of her. And if someone were to spill their drink on it, destroying the picture, I'd be a little annoyed, perhaps even upset at the loss. This is *valuable* because she made it.

2.5 The Heart's Own Reasons

Another parent who has never met my daughter and has no particular interest in her will likely find the painting unremarkable – I can be aware of this fact despite the significance the painting has for me. Even if the other parent thinks it is a nice enough painting, it will not have the same significance for them as it does for me. For me, the painting is an episode in a relationship, it is a form of contact with my beloved. For the other parent, it's nothing of the sort, and if it is spoiled or destroyed, that's nothing to get upset about. It's just another painting by just another child. My experience of the painting is different from the other parent's in a number of ways. I attach a significance to the painting itself, but also the experience of looking at it fills me with joy. I see things in it that the other parent doesn't, and I see it *as* something that the other parent doesn't.

Pascal may well have something like Psalm 19 in mind when thinking of the sky and the birds:

> The heavens declare the glory of God; the skies proclaim the work of his hands.

We can imagine that David, the shepherd and psalmist, full of love for God the maker of the world, looked up at the sky and saw God's glory declared. And we can imagine an atheist beside him (one of the sheep, Pascal might say), thinking that though the sky looks glorious maybe, there is nothing there that indicates that it is a declaration of *God's* glory, or a declaration of any kind at all. The "grammar" of the sky is third-personal, as it were, rather than a second-personal communication – an *It* rather than a *Thou* to use Martin Buber's terms. This, I suggest, is just the distinction between the parents and the painting in my earlier example. And if we ask the atheist, "Do you think David is hallucinating?" the atheist could reasonably reply, "No, he's just assigning the sky a significance that is misplaced because of the feelings he has." The *content* isn't different – both see the same blue sky – but the *manner* in which they each see is different. And this can have enormous significance for the shepherd's life. If it also is significant to the atheist, because seeing something beautiful is significant, it is at any rate a different significance.

So the heart can clearly alter the significance that we assign to things. And this significance amounts to a difference in *how things look*, and how things look can determine what reasons one has. It just *looks* to David like the sky is declaring something, but not to the atheist. It is not something that David infers, it is a feature of his experience. This does not mean that the content is different – it does not mean that one person is blind or that the other is hallucinating.[10] Rather, they see things as if they live in different worlds. Or, to put it a bit differently, we live differently in the world according to our hearts (S187/L154-5).

We can take the idea that the world looks different to people with different states of heart quite literally, then. And we can see how it might solve the problem of the ambiguity of the world, or divine hiddenness. For those who love God, everything in the world and in nature takes on the significance of having been made by God. For those who do not love God, there is no such significance in anything. But each could acknowledge the other's experience, just as you might acknowledge the significance that I assign a painting even if you think, to yourself, that I'm delusional, that I actually have no child who painted it. The problem in such a case is not *my experience*. The problem is the misfiring in my heart, a false belief that I have a child, and some misplaced passions. You can still acknowledge the significance it has for me, even if you think that significance is misplaced.

Relatedly, the significance that the sky has for David is not, as philosophers like to say, *epistemically* significant for his belief that God exists. Suppose again that you doubted that I have a child at all, but realized that I was convinced of it and that I was swooning over what I thought was her painting. Could I convince you that I have a child by appealing to the existence of the painting? No, because you already accept that there is a painting there, you just don't think it was created in the way I think it was (by my child). Could I convince you by appealing to the way I feel when I look at it, or by the significance the experience has for me? No, because you already accept that I believe this is my child's painting, and that I feel these (misplaced) feelings

---

[10] There is a question about whether the significance, as I am putting it, figures into the content of the experience itself. Here I am using "content" to mean merely the veridicality conditions of the experience, or the conditions under which the experience is veridical rather than a hallucination. Whether such high-level content as "this declares God's glory" is part of the very content is a theoretical question about perception that I do not aim to settle here.

2.5 *The Heart's Own Reasons*

accordingly. So the appeal to the painting is bound to fail to convince you – bound to "arouse contempt" (S644/L781) as Pascal would say of those who appeal to signs of God in nature. But *for myself*, given what I feel and believe about the painting, it is proof "in a sense" (S38/L3) of my child. That she painted something of course implies that she exists! Why is this proof only "in a sense," though?

We saw in the two earlier essays, discussed in Chapter 1, that Pascal recognized two different senses, or uses, of proof: a proof of something you already know, and a proof you use to convince someone of something. Perhaps the sky and birds are proof in the first sense, but not in the send sense. But "in a sense" in S38/L3 goes much deeper, I think.

For Pascal, who here was following Augustine, the heart or the love of God preceded any understanding of God.[11] In order to see the sky as declaring God's glory in the first place, you must already have an inclined heart, a heart that loves the creator of the sky. But if you love God, and in virtue of this relationship see the world as His work, you cannot then go on to infer that God exists on the basis of how things look. That love already assumes his existence. So, although the fact that the sky looks like it declares God's glory suggests that God exists, just as God's creation implies that God created it and therefore exists, this is only proof "in a sense." You take it to be God's creation only because you already love God.

Pascal was careful to grant that experience of the world as divinely made is not a good proof for the dialectical purpose of convincing the unbeliever, and this was his aim, so he did not dwell on any such "proof" for long. But something symmetrical, and often overlooked, applies to the atheist's experience, the experience of the world as undivine, a heartless mechanism: if you see the world as entirely uninspiring and unworthy of being the work of God, that is "proof" that there is no God only in a sense as well. It is only due to your heart, which lacks any love of the divine, and only loves worldly things, that you see things in the world as ungodly. This point is easily lost in heated debates about God.

---

[11] Along these lines, Augustine wrote: "Charity, the love of God, gives access to an understanding, wisdom, that transcends the insights of the pure intellect" (*De Trinitate*, 352); "Unless we love Him now, we shall never see Him. But who loves that which he does not know?" (*De Trinitate*, 8.4.6); "Therefore, the more ardently we love God, so much the more certainly and calmly do we see Him" (8.9.13).

Look, the atheist says, all there is here is just a bunch of atoms and electrons crashing around! The reply should be: that's how it looks to you, but to me it looks like the mechanics of a brilliant edifice created by God – a God whom we betrayed, but by grace those who love him can see this plain truth. The atoms declare God's glory! If the world seems unholy, and you can find no sign of God here, it is only because your heart is in the wrong place:

> What shall we conclude from all our obscurities, then, if not our unworthiness? (S690/L445)

The fact that the world looks Godly to some is not an effective *proof* that there is a God; likewise the fact that the world looks ungodly to others is not an effective proof against God either, especially against a *hidden* God as Pascal's theology has it. The way things look might confirm what each has in their hearts – proof "in a sense" – but it is not enough to prove anything to those without the same heart. In the next chapter, we will look more closely at this solution to the hiddenness (to some) of God. But in the big picture, this is just another instance of what we've seen before, that experience and proof do not *themselves* establish much. We can see now that this is because what significance experience has is due to the heart. The heart has its own reasons; the heart operates in an entirely different order from the order of reason (S329/L298).

The Pascalian conception of seeing God in nature, or rather seeing nature as Godly, as a result of experiencing it under the influence of the right state of heart, has great potential to inform discussions of religious experience today. For the most part, contemporary discussions of religious experience emphasize the *content* of the experience. They typically model religious experience on perceptual experience, where in religious experience one perceives God's action as part of the content of what one experiences.[12] But if we understand religious experience as I am suggesting Pascal understood it, we can come to see religious experience less as a special mystical, direct interaction with God, and more as a manner of seeing the world, as God's. This undermines its *epistemological*

---

[12] Two prominent examples are Alston, William P. (1991). *Perceiving God: The Epistemology of Religious Experience*. Ithaca, New York: Cornell University Press, and Plantinga, Alvin (2000). Religious belief as "properly basic." In Brian Davies (ed.), *Philosophy of Religion: A Guide and Anthology*. New York: Oxford University Press.

2.5 The Heart's Own Reasons

significance as *evidence* for God, as we've just seen. But it still can serve as an indication or manifestation of the strength of one's devotion.[13] It is well worth reconsidering these different approaches to religious experience, especially since the Pascalian conception seems much more common, and therefore more relevant to the actual practice of religion.

Let us sum up. We have an affective faculty, one that loves, fears, wills, is attracted, and is repulsed, which consequently determines the range of things one can believe and even how we see things. The human heart always is ready to believe, with full certainty and clarity, the first principles of geometry. And it is hardened against the belief that this is all one long dream. But some human hearts are hardened against God, while others are inclined toward God – both the belief that there is a God, and toward God himself, in the sense of loving Him. Neither "rationalist" nor "empiricist" really makes for a good description of such a view. It is a "heartist" view, or a *cordate* epistemology. The heart is not *merely* a disposition, because it determines what reasons you have and can respond to.

Not all states of the heart are equal: only one kind of heart enables us to be great, as we will soon see. The heart is not merely at the center of Pascal's epistemology, though it may seem that way since so far in this book we have focused on belief. We will see that just as the heart is the key to seeing and believing things rightly, it is also the key to a good life and greatness for humans, a greatness beyond the order of body and reason. Though we are all born with a certain heart, since the Fall, each of us can choose to seek out a different heart, one that is oriented toward God. Our dignity lies in our thought. But our potential greatness lies in the heart, which defines the arena in which thought operates.

---

[13] Such was the view of religious experience of St. Teresa of Avila, a mystic who also regarded her experiences as epistemically irrelevant, except as a measure of her devotion to God. See Williams, Rowan. (2000). *Teresa of Avila*. Continuum International Publishing Group, p. 147 ff.

CHAPTER 3

The Ambiguous World

Pascal's world is ambiguous. One can look at it and see nothing but a heartless mechanism, or one can look at it and see God's will manifested in creation, throbbing with love.[1] Reality is amenable to these different interpretations. It can look one way if you don't love God, and it can look another very different way if you do love God. The world is like a holographic sheet, appearing to be in different postures depending on the angle of viewing.

This is an important aspect of Pascal's view, but not just because it provides a defense against the sort of atheist argument that claims that if God existed, then it would be obvious to everyone who looks around at creation. Pascal takes it further than that: the fact that the world is amenable to these different interpretations is itself a piece of evidence about reality that confirms Christianity to the exclusion of other religions. Pascal argues this repeatedly and in different ways throughout the *Pensées*. In this chapter, we explore this idea and consider how far it can be made plausible, and what this might tell us about the sort of confirmation Pascal had in mind.

Whether we have evidence for Christianity in the world's ambiguity is of course a matter of great interest itself. But the structure of this debate, and the way in which ambiguity is used to make sense of differing positions, is also a useful idea in other contexts. Take, for instance, our current political moment. We live in contentious and polarizing times. Pascal's insights can be applied to various disagreements in our society, which makes his ideas particularly relevant today. Insofar as the world can appear differently to different people – and we

---

[1] Malcolm (ibid.).

will see that there is good reason to believe that Pascal was right about this – one can accept that one's adversary in a debate is being reasonable at least in the sense that they are following the evidence available to them given their state. This perspectival approach to disagreement, while enabling us to reject dogmatism by practicing intellectual humility, avoids relativism if developed correctly. We will see that a good Pascalian view still entails that there are objective facts about the world and our situation in it, and that there is even a basis on this view for evaluating which perspectives (and conclusions) are better and best.

3.1 The Metaphysical Significance of Ambiguity

Since Pascal wanted to convince his readers to love God, his first step was to try to understand why people don't already love God. There was a readily available and simple explanation for this: when you look at the world, it isn't at all obvious that it was created by God. So, where is God? This much is understandable, and even predictable according to Pascal's religion. But some take this to be a refutation of Christianity, since they assume that Christianity implies that the existence of God should be plainly obvious to all.

The first step in Pascal's handling of the issue is, as we saw in the previous chapter, to show that the ambiguity of the world, "hiddenness," is not a refutation of Christianity. In this chapter, it is worth going into a little more detail on this point, in order to understand all of its implications. Those who mistakenly think that ambiguity contradicts Christianity simply don't understand Christianity:

> Let them at least learn what is the religion they attack, before they attack it. If this religion boasted of having a clear view of God and of possessing it openly and unveiled, to say that we see nothing in the world proving it so clearly would be to attack it. But this religion says, on the contrary, that men are in darkness and estranged from God, that he has hidden himself from their knowledge – this is even the name he is given in the Scriptures: The Hidden God. If indeed it strives equally to establish these two things: that God has established visible signs in the Church by which those who would sincerely seek him can know him, and nevertheless so disguised them that he will be perceived only by those who seek him with all their heart, then what advantage can they derive when, in their

carelessness, as they profess to be searching for the truth, they cry out that nothing reveals it to them? For that darkness in which they exist and with which they reproach the Church merely establishes one of the things this religion affirms without affecting the other, and, far from destroying its doctrine, establishes it. (S681/L427)

Only those who *truly seek* can complain that either Christianity is false or else God has abandoned them by refusing His grace. But many nonbelievers in Pascal's day, and in ours, have not genuinely tried to seek God:

> They think they have made great efforts to learn when they have spent a few hours reading some book of Scripture and questioned a priest on the truths of the faith. After that, they boast that they have searched without success in books and among men. (S681/L427)

This nonbeliever has no right, then, to claim that Christianity is false, because they have not *genuinely* sought God.

Instead, understood correctly, Christianity has as an essential feature that the world will seem Godly to some and not others:

> We understand nothing of God's works, unless we take as a principle that he wanted to blind some people and enlighten others. (S264/L232)

> Wanting to appear openly to those who seek him with all their heart and hidden from those who flee him with all their heart, God has tempered the knowledge of himself by giving signs of himself that are visible to those who seek him, and not by those who do not seek him. There is enough light for those who desire only to see and enough darkness for those of a contrary disposition. (S274/L149)

But Pascal goes further: not only does ambiguity fail to refute Christianity, it confirms it and places it above all other religions, including Deism and the God of the philosophers. These are some short, representative samples on this point:

> God being thus hidden, any religion that does not say God is hidden is not true. And any religion that does not explain it is not instructive. Our religion does all this. Truly you are a hidden God. (S274/L149)

> ... What can be seen [in the world] indicates neither the complete absence, nor the obvious presence of divinity, but the presence of a God who hides himself. Everything carries this stamp. (S690/L438-50)

3.1 The Metaphysical Significance of Ambiguity

What we can see by observing ourselves and our relation to the world is that things are ambiguous, that the world is capable of being seen in different ways, depending on the affective perspective of the human viewer. That the world is capable of being seen in these different ways confirms Christianity, because it is the only religion that says that God will be hidden to those without the love of God in their hearts. Other religions say things inconsistent with this, at least on Pascal's understanding of them.

We can imagine, for example, that a pagan religion implies that there is, say, a river spirit and a sky spirit. But the river can dry up or be polluted, and so is not worthy of worship and at any rate when we look at it, it doesn't necessarily or obviously look *divine*, it does not look to be from an order of things beyond us or the material world. Same with the sky: the sky can look dull, drab, and certainly uninspiring. On a monotheistic religion which does not include the theology of the Fall, God made the world. But the world does not obviously look God-made; this is no paradise. Sure, we could blame some of nature's corruption on human activity, but not all of it. Nature seems imperfect, and therefore undivine. Deism and the God of the philosophers suffer from a similar problem. If God is a universal being who made all of this, and if God is a perfect, abstract being, we should see some evidence of this in nature. There should be evidence of a *perfect* world, if a perfect God made it just the way He wanted it.

Instead, what we find in the world is the "stamp" of a God who hides himself from some while at the same time revealing himself to others, to those with faith and love in their hearts. Why? Because we have already betrayed him, and in his compassion he gives us each a chance to redeem ourselves. Most don't genuinely try, though, so they are never redeemed.

Considered from a different angle, this can be understood straightforwardly as a sort of argument for theism – to be clear, Pascal was explicitly aiming to convince people to become Catholics, so he would not have put it this way. But let us zoom out a bit and consider a more general argument inspired by Pascal. Could the world, by which I mean nature on earth and in the universe, including all the large and little things like humans, insects, clouds, and nebula, have looked like a bunch of disjointed, random, disgusting, or just flatly uninspired crap? Could the sky, as seen from here, for example, have looked not glorious at all, so that not even a true believer would think that it declares God's glory? It seems pretty plausible that the answer is Yes; the world could have failed to have been such as to appear divine to those who feel love for what they take to be its creator in their hearts. But then the fact that our world *is* capable of being viewed in this way, that it is such as to look, from at least one perspective, divine or Godly, is some evidence that it is indeed divine or Godly. Otherwise, why is nature magnificent and beautiful? If it weren't the world of a god, we should expect that it wouldn't look to be, even to those with the right state of heart. Are we to guess that this is some sort of coincidence?

Of course, this is no "proof." It's just some suggestion or reason in favor of the hypothesis that the world was created by something like a god, something such that when you love it, the world takes on a significance relating to it. And that is simply because the probability that it would look like this to lovers of the creator if that weren't the case seems somewhat low. The world *could* have been such that those who want to love its creator see nothing inspiring in it that aids their pursuit of that desire. But we see that it is not that way, since it is ambiguous. We can anticipate some objections to this, and I think they are instructive, not only philosophically in general but also because they indicate how rich these Pascalian ideas are.

Perhaps the most obvious objection comes from a reflection on why a subject with the right love in their heart might experience the world as divine. The objection is that the world could *seem* to be Godly to those with the right love in their hearts, even if there is no God or creator and even if nature is not objectively lovely. This could come from one of two directions. In one scenario, we could have evolved to have this aesthetic and spiritual sensation when beholding nature – however nature objectively is – because it is somehow an advantageous adaptation to be like that, or else being susceptible to such experience is a by-product of something else about our brains that is an advantageous adaptation.

Maybe that is correct, and we evolved for some reason or other to be susceptible to seeing the world as Godly when we are sufficiently effusive in our hearts. Certainly this is not a culturally specific thing – the ancients expressed their reverence for nature, as do people from all over the world. Suppose we accept the fact that humans evolved this

3.1 The Metaphysical Significance of Ambiguity

capacity to see nature, however it is objectively, as sublime in a way that inspires religious fervor. If the fact that this capacity is the product of evolution debunks the conclusion we draw from the exercise of this capacity, then it should also debunk almost everything else we conclude by exercising our capacities. Our sensory apparatus, after all, also evolved by a process of selection that was not primarily sensitive to accuracy. What matters, from an evolutionary standpoint, is the transmission of genes not the generation of correct beliefs that enhance our understanding of the truth about the world. Our moral sense, too, must have evolved (along with everything else), but philosophers debate (even today) whether this fact successfully debunks our moral attitudes. So, the verdict on this objection is unclear, or at least not obvious.[2]

The other direction from which an objection might be launched is not from the subject side of the experience, but from the object. The world itself could have been generated or ordered in a way that it is, emotionally and aesthetically speaking, indistinguishable to our experience from a creator that is worthy of our love, but without ever having been created by any such God. That it might be a personal God who made all of this, and that those who revere it can see this most clearly, might be a sort of anthropomorphic response we have to the basic creative force of the universe. After all, we are told by physicists today that certain symmetries and constants must be just so in order for life to have any possibility of evolving.[3] Perhaps those constraints are structurally elegant in a way that suggests to the feeble and arbitrarily evolved human mind that it is worthy of love. If the world was made of a bunch of random and disjointed crap, how could it also be stable enough for us to have evolved?

Maybe so. But if the principle that generates the world is so easily mistaken, at least in our clouded minds, for God, in that it inspires these feelings of reverence, then how distinct is it from God or a god's work? Clearly we cannot know, we are betting, with this objection, that

---

[2] For a somewhat similar move, see Plantinga's evolutionary argument against naturalism in Plantinga, Alvin (1993). *Warrant and Proper Function*. Oxford: Oxford University Press, ch. 12. For a classic formulation of the evolutionary debunking argument in ethics, see Street, Sharon (2006). A Darwinian dilemma for realist theories of value. *Philosophical Studies* 127 (1): 109–166.
[3] This is the basis of the so-called fine-tuning argument. See Rees, Martin J. (2001). *Just Six Numbers*. New York: Basic Books.

nothing else about these principles or what ties them together is godlike or implies a God. More on this bet will be discussed in Chapter 5.

One last note about this issue is in order. This argument for some sort of creator of nature is distinct from any "design" argument. In a design argument, one observes some complexity or order in nature, and on the basis of an assumption that this implies that nature was designed infers that there must have been a designer of nature. Such arguments rely on a principle about complexity and order, and what is required to generate them. But our argument does not appeal to any such principle. Rather, it appeals to an immediate, affective response to the world, and so it is more Pascalian (Pascal himself rejected the design argument as he did the other metaphysical "proofs").

That the universe is capable of being interpreted in the way that David does when he sees the sky declaring God's glory is a significant fact about it, or us, or both. For Pascal this disconfirmed a lot of other religions, and confirmed his. But he recognized this alone would not convince anyone of God, let alone of the Fall. He relied, instead, on how perfectly the Fall describes our situation, and how much better suited we are to believing the Fall than remaining in our corrupted state (the topic of the next Chapter).

3.2 Disagreement (of Hearts and Minds), Rationality, and Non-relativism

Just as Pascal's God (the God of the Bible and the Fall) is distinct in important ways from the philosopher's God (the impersonal being with all perfections), Pascal's conception of how we might disagree with each other about God is also distinct from the familiar three-part distinction of standard philosophy of religion.

The standard three-part distinction is between theists, who believe in God, atheists, who believe there is no God, and agnostics, who suspend judgment on the matter. As a description of possible doxastic attitudes toward God, this looks to be exhaustive.

But there is another, and in some ways more philosophically fruitful, way of understanding the three-part distinction. Rather than focusing on what we believe, focus on what we think there is evidence for. A theist is one who thinks that there is sufficient evidence to make

3.2 Disagreement, Rationality, and Non-relativism

belief that God exists rational, and an atheist thinks there is sufficient evidence to make belief that God doesn't exist rational. Unless they go in for relativism of some sort, each thinks the other is wrong, either because they believe something unsupported by the evidence or because they have failed to appreciate what the real evidence is. The agnostic, on this way of carving up the territory, thinks that we lack evidence to make either belief rational. This means that there is insufficient evidence that there is a God, and insufficient evidence that there is no God. This was the original definition of the term "agnostic" when it was coined in the nineteenth century by T. H. Huxley, to denote people who, "like [himself], confess themselves to be hopelessly ignorant concerning a variety of matters, about which metaphysicians and theologians, both orthodox and heterodox, dogmatize with the utmost confidence."[4] On one way of understanding this not only does the agnostic assess that she lacks sufficient evidence either way but she also holds that we could never possibly have sufficient evidence, because we are *hopelessly* ignorant about this matter.

The feature of agnosticism that I just described, that no foreseeable evidence will ever be sufficient to justify either belief in God or belief that there is no God, is an important feature of the position. Without it, one could claim to be an agnostic before one ever considered any evidence either way. Such a disinterested person thinks that her own evidence is insufficient, because she's never bothered to look or think of any. But she is of course importantly different, philosophically, from a principled agnostic who has reflected on the limitations of human cognition and concluded that knowledge of such things as God's existence (or nonexistence) is impossible. We can say, then, that someone who simply hasn't considered the matter, and for that reason lacks sufficient evidence either way, is *uninterested*, rather than an agnostic. So we have a standard trio of positions described. Each of the three thinks that the other two are wrong in the sense that they have misconstrued the quality of the evidence.

There is also another character that we are all familiar with today: the relativist. The relativist, perhaps out of a desire to make peace between

---

[4] Huxley, Thomas Henry (1884). Agnosticism: A symposium. In Charles Watts (ed.), *The Agnostic Annual*. London: Charles Watts. pp. 5–6.

the various parties, says that each person is right in their own way. "You are right *for you*," the relativist says to each of them. According to the relativist, there is no absolute or neutral truth about which of the three positions is best. There is only the fact that each person holds the position that is best for themselves. No one is *objectively* doing anything wrong.

Pascal's ideas transcend the standard trio of positions without descending into relativism. Pascal himself is a theist, and he thinks there is overwhelming evidence that God exists: just look around, and you see God's work everywhere. Pascal's God does not expect us to believe in Him on blind faith or without reason, but nor does Pascal's God want to "subdue you by tyranny" (S182/L149). This means that there isn't overwhelming or sufficient evidence in the world to rationally compel the atheist to switch teams and believe in God, but there is sufficient evidence in the world to make belief in God reasonable. How is this possible, if both are looking at the same world? Because how you see the world, and so what evidence you have, depends on your heart, and the two have different hearts. This is why the sky and birds prove God for some, but not others. So the theist need not think that the atheist or the agnostic is being *irrational* or *unreasonable* in the sense of failing to respond to evidence. Instead, the theist should think that they are benighted in another way: their heart is in the wrong place, and so they aren't seeing things in the best way they could. This isn't a problem or deficit of *rationality* and assessment of evidence. It is a passional deficit of the heart. They're living the wrong kind of life, they want and love the wrong things, and their fundamental orientation is off. But – and this is crucially important – Pascal is not thereby buying into any sort of relativism. There *is* an objectively correct way to be, and that's to have your heart in the right place and be a theist. How can you know that this is the right way for your heart to be, unless you're already a theist? This pressing question will have to wait for Chapter 5.

The suggestion here is not that anything goes. In the physical order of things, reasonable conclusions are of course constrained by our natural starting points, the first principles, and our experience. Pascal was, after all, an accomplished empirical scientist, having experimentally confirmed the existence of the vacuum. He understood that beliefs about the world must be tested against the evidence. In general, our reasoning

3.2 Disagreement, Rationality, and Non-relativism 81

and conclusions don't exist in a vacuum. He did not deny that we learn about the world empirically and in an objective way. But all experiencing, and all thinking, is also conditioned by the heart, so that no point of view is neutral or blank, it is all motivated. In a disagreement between the theist and the atheist, we have a clash of hearts and incommensurable experiences – they are effectively responding to *different sets of evidence* – but this is not to say that any claim about the world whatsoever can be justified. The world cannot appear to be *any* which way, it is not *maximally* ambiguous. And at any rate, not all states of heart, and so not all ways of seeing the world, are equal or equally correct. The heart should love only what is worthy of love, *objectively* worthy given the nature of humans and where we came from, and given who in fact created the world.

Pascal held that the best thing to do for an atheist or agnostic is to *seek* God (we will get into exactly what makes this reasonable in Chapter 5, when we consider the famous "wager"). But if a person is seeking and still hasn't found God, or hasn't discovered a love of God in the heart, that person is still unhappy and in an objectively bad situation. They are like someone who wants to fall in love and hasn't found anyone to love yet. And a person who doesn't even seek is of course in a bad place too, but Pascal did not think that their problem was one of rationality, or that they were mismanaging their evidence, as today's apologists often hold. The badness of their situation concerns their heart, and the objective situation – that they are corrupted, post-Fall humans – not their mind. To the extent that such atheists fail to "think well," it is because they have not considered yet the limits of their reason, that what they see in the world may be limited in scope, since it is just one possible perspective. But given the evidence that they are in a position to appreciate from this flawed state, their (non)belief is justified by their available evidence.

We should not overstate this point for Pascal, as he also offered concrete ways in which the atheists fail to live up to their own standards of clarity, for example in S193/L161. In fact, he calls the atheists who do not seek *foolish*:

> There are only three kinds of people: those who serve God, having found him; those who are busy seeking him, not having found him; those who

live without seeking or finding him. The first are reasonable and happy, the last are foolish and unhappy; those in the middle are unhappy and reasonable. (S192/L160)

One of the standard arguments taught in philosophy of religion classes is St. Anselm's "Ontological" argument, which is a proof of God's existence of exactly the sort that Pascal rejects. The point of departure for the proof, which is supposed to convince the atheist, is Psalm 14:1, "the fool says in his heart, 'there is no God'." Anselm then aims to show how the thought that there is no God is incoherent (since, roughly, the concept of God is a concept of something that exists). It is instructive to notice that Pascal, who rejects the idea that the standoff with the atheist is one stemming from reason, takes an entirely different approach to understanding this "foolishness." The atheist is foolish for not seeking God in her heart, but not because there is a contradiction to the thought that there is no God (even if there is one). Rather, the non-seeking atheist is foolish, and "unreasonable," because her *heart* is not in the right place yet she doesn't seek to make it right. She thinks everything is fine, and that the way she sees things is the best way, but in fact she is fully corrupted and not seeing things as they are. The famous "wager" is supposed to show why, exactly, this is unreasonable.

So far we have neglected the agnostic. For Pascal, *something* is right about the agnostic's position. There is not sufficient evidence in the world to justify belief, either in theism or atheism, *without the heart being in the right place*. Or, at least, belief in God without love of God in the heart is useless for salvation. But the agnostic is misrepresenting the situation. Pascal's view is that reason gives us nothing by itself without the heart, so this is just an instance of a general skeptical principle that we can know nothing without the heart, so that the state of one's heart determines the limits of what one can know. Furthermore, the agnostic is guilty of being too passive, too willing to give up on belief. Being "too docile in belief" is "a natural vice, like incredulity, and just as pernicious" (S219/L187).

The notion that some people are just too timid in their belief, so concerned with avoiding error that they lose sight of the value of believing true and important things, is a familiar one from William James' *The Will to Belief*, which seems largely inspired by Pascal. The

3.2 Disagreement, Rationality, and Non-relativism

way James developed the idea people have different "passional natures" which lead them to either be more skeptical or more adventurous in their inquiry. When it comes to matters that are in principle beyond the capacity of intellect to judge, as in matters of religion, both dispositions are equally "rational," or rather prerational. The agnostic, even if her nonbelief fits well with her lack of evidence, wrongly surmises that sufficient evidence is *impossible*. We are not *hopelessly* ignorant, as Huxley said. We are, rather, ignorant so long as we lack hope, but if our hearts were in the right place, we'd have plenty of evidence.

Pascal has managed to carve out a position that is hard to categorize in the standard way of doing philosophy of religion, and it has potential to upend the standard debates. To emphasize again, this is not relativism. Objectively speaking, the right way to be is to love God and thereby see signs of God everywhere in the world. As Genesis describes it, God made the world, so wherever you look you are seeing God's work. Furthermore, the world itself is, objectively, ambiguous. And another objective fact about it is *why* it is ambiguous: because of the Fall. This entails, objectively, that humans are created by God, and that we are miserable and corrupt, and can only be saved by the grace of God. Instead of relativism, we have a sort of toleration and understanding of the nonbeliever, a recognition that they are responding to the evidence that they can access in their current state. It is perspectivist, not relativist, because while it accepts that the world appears differently depending on how the heart is, there is only one world, and one correct way to be and believe.

How do we help the nonbelievers, then? The root of the nonbelievers' resistance is not a lack of evidence, it is a hardening of their hearts. So to change their minds we must appeal to their hearts:

> Men despise religion; they hate it and fear that it is true. To cure this, we must begin by showing that religion is not contrary to reason, but worthy of veneration and respect. Next we must make it attractive, to make the good wish it were true, and then we must show that it is true.
> Worthy of veneration because it has properly understood man.
> Attractive because it promises the true good. (S46/L12)

The way you encourage someone to love something is by making it attractive. To change their minds, you cannot simply try to shove more evidence in their faces; the theist cannot appeal to the evidence they see of God everywhere:

> [F]or those in whom this light is extinguished and in whom we are trying to rekindle it, these people destitute of faith and grace, who, seeking with all their light whatever they see in nature that can lead them to this knowledge, find only obscurity and darkness; to tell them that they have only to look at the smallest things surrounding them to see God openly ... is to give them ground for believing that the proofs of our religion are indeed weak. And I see by reason and experience that nothing is more calculated to arouse their contempt. (S644/L781)

Instead, we must convince them to try to seek to change their hearts, to make them wish religion were true, to stop them hating it. How can we do this? Perhaps by being an example, perhaps by presenting them with a religious picture of the world, or of human life. Pascal takes up the work of trying to show the nonbeliever that human nature without God is doomed – we will see how he argues this, and how well he describes our problems today, in the next chapter. For now the point is that presenting someone whose heart is in the wrong place with more evidence, more arguments, more disagreement is useless. This is, in my estimation, an important insight of potentially *enormous* consequence for us especially today. The idea – which we saw in Chapter 1 when discussing *The Art of Persuasion* – is that in order to convince someone, one must take into account the ambiguity of the world, and the fact that people see in things what their heart tempts them to see. This applies fully generally, not just in matters of religion:

> When we want to correct another usefully and show him he is wrong, we must notice from what side he takes up the matter, for from that side it is usually true; and we must admit that truth to him, but show him the side from which it is false. This will satisfy him, for he will see that he was not wrong and merely failed to see all sides. Now, we are not offended at not seeing everything, but we do not like to be wrong. Perhaps this comes from the fact that man by nature cannot see everything, and that by nature he cannot be wrong from the side he takes up, since our sense perceptions are always true. (S579/L701)

Notice that this is exactly what Pascal has painstakingly done in his own work: he has admitted and described in detail that God seems to be absent to those without faith, that the problem of hiddenness is real because the nonbeliever will not see God's work everywhere. Instead, they will see nothing but a world that inspires "doubt and confusion." He is admitting that the world can seem that way, that the world is ambiguous. But he wants to tell us: you are not seeing *everything*, only part of the world of the Fall. You haven't seen things through God-tinted glasses yet. You should at least try to.

We can fruitfully apply this same insight to topics outside of religion, and thereby gain an understanding of our current social and political situation.

3.3 Echo Chambers and Conspiracy Theories: A Pascalian Perspective

Today's world is a deeply fragmented one. Though we all live in the same world and have access to the same vast system of information, we have reached vastly different conclusions, both individually and as groups. Pascal was struck by the same kind of fragmentation: seeing the same world, some are absolutely faithful, and others so ready to dismiss God that they choose a "libertine," secular path.

"Truth is so obscure in these times, and falsehood so well established," wrote Pascal, "that, unless we loved the truth, we could not know it" (S617/L739). He could have written this today, noticing that anyone who wants an accurate picture of things must evade misinformation, conspiracy theories, and targeted news feeds that present material that is tailor-made to the viewer's biases. It is easier than ever to see what we prefer to see, given how plentiful and accessible information is. Whether on the left or the right, an online reader is exposed primarily to either sources saying something that resonates with what they are looking for, or commentary on sources with unfriendly information that encourages the reader to mistrust it. While this sort of dynamic has always been the case to some extent, the technological situation puts our biases on industrial strength steroids, and with computerized precision and relentlessness. The result is excessive polarization and disagreement even about the basic facts, as the charges of "fake news" and misinformation are weaponized to minimize the chances of giving another perspective a chance. One must really love truth, indeed, to make the enormous effort to see through all of this. And one must love truth more than the love (and hate) that motivates one to be on the left or the right in the first place.

Consider a climate change denier (choose a different example if that one is inconvenient). Such a person thinks that all the climatologist reports and all the scientific studies are fabricated. The scientists, so this person has been convinced, are being bribed by the liberal politicians who, for personal gain (or perhaps under foreign influence?), want everyone to believe there is a looming climate catastrophe, so that we will all stop using fossil fuels. This is a sort of conspiracy theory, because a group of malevolent actors are conspiring to trick us, and they are cleverly producing misleading "evidence" to throw most of us off track. Those of us who have figured it out, though, know that this is all fake evidence. Now, what happens when you present such a person with *more* evidence for climate change? You are then simply reinforcing part of their theory: that the conspirators are producing misleading evidence. So how do we engage with such a person, and how can they ever change their minds?

A disagreement with such a person may seem intractable. If you present them with more evidence, they'll just entrench. If you explain to them why you don't believe what they do, they have a ready explanation: you've been duped. Why are you so sure, they might ask, that you are the one who is being rational, and that we (the deniers) are the crazy ones?

The believer of this sort of conspiracy theory is likely to get information from other believers, their social media will be filled with material from their network of mostly like-minded people who will encourage each other to ignore or explain away any information that is inconvenient to their shared worldview. In other words, such people often find themselves in echo chambers that reinforce the belief, whether their belief brought them into the echo chamber in the first place or vice versa. Perhaps some other common interests, fears, or loves brought them into online contact with a community, which then indoctrinated them into the conspiracy theory. Perhaps this community just happens to be the available friend. Sometimes, tragically, people are radicalized in this way. The more dug in a person is, socially surrounded by an echo

3.3 Echo Chambers and Conspiracy Theories

chamber that amplifies the theory, the harder it becomes to get through to them.

There is a lot to say about the psychology and epistemology of echo chambers and conspiracy theories. It is a commonplace, though, that this situation, and the kinds of disagreements within society that it leads to, is key to polarization and other social phenomena that define (some would say that are wrecking) our political culture. So, this is one of the most pressing issues of our day. What I want to suggest here is that a Pascalian epistemology offers a unique perspective on how to analyze such disagreements and how to approach resolving them.

Before diving into how to convince the conspiracy believers, a Pascalian hesitation is in order. One thing Pascal cautioned about was intellectual arrogance. He thought that, in matters of the world, we should not rush to conclusions. This falls directly out of his epistemology. The fact is that you, the lone citizen with access to the internet and the news, cannot figure out exactly what is going on because you cannot follow every line of inquiry into the reliability of every source, and you cannot be an expert in everything. You cannot go it alone. There is too much noise in the signals you can receive. You should therefore not act rashly based on the view that appeals to you most, and you should be humble, for the simple fact that you could be wrong, and those like you have been wrong before.

> How many things have telescopes revealed to us that did not exist for our past philosophers! We sincerely represented Holy Scripture on the great number of stars by saying, "There are only 1,022 of them; we know it."
>
> "There is grass on the earth; we see it. From the moon we would not see it. And on this grass are filaments, and in these filaments small animals; but after that, nothing more?" O presumptuous man!
>
> "Mixtures are composed of elements; and the elements not?" O presumptuous man! Here is a delicate point. We must not say that there is something we do not see. We must then talk like others, but not think like them. (S645/L782)

And this is not merely because of the incapacity of our reason and experience to determine the ultimate nature of things but also because to see things is to see things from a perspective, and there are always other available perspectives. These perspectives include the state of one's heart, but also one's specific situation in the world, one's age, one's social position, and even how much one has thought about things, which can have a warping effect on the outcomes of inquiry. "Not thinking enough or thinking too much about things makes us stubborn and opinionated" (S55/L21). So, in the first place, Pascal teaches open-mindedness.

But when it comes to handling active disagreement, as in the case of climate change, what does this approach suggest? Pascalian epistemology analyzes the disagreement at least in part by assuming that the world, the facts, the reports, and the news simply look different and have different significance to those with different motivations. In other words, Pascalian epistemology first focuses on the ways in which your motivations affect what you see and how you reason about it. If your heart is faithful to, say, a coal country political organization, you will despise sources that make claims that are dissonant with the interests of coal country. And when you step out into an unseasonably hot Autumn day, you will focus on the fact that there have always been irregular weather patterns, not the fact that this is unusually warm. When a Democratic politician makes a speech urging investment in renewable sources of energy, they will just *seem* to be a lying, sleezy politician. Just look at that smile, you think to yourself, he's so fake! When presented with graphs correlating carbon levels in the atmosphere and global temperatures, you'll think very critically and engage in an inquiry into what is wrong with the data (or else you'll dismiss the whole thing as propaganda). When you hear, on your TikTok feed, someone say that a volcano puts more carbon into the atmosphere than all of human activity ever has in hundreds of years, you'll believe it uncritically with no investigation. This is the familiar phenomenon of motivated reasoning, and a Pascalian will tend to explain the conspiracy theorist's beliefs accordingly. None of this is to say, of course, that there is no objectively better way to respond to these facts.

At the root of the problem, insofar as this belief is a problem, is the person's heart. The problem could be that they love the coal country politician because they love coal country. Perhaps that is where they're from, or it represents a pure and just America to them. And like-hearted people find each other (very easily online especially), support each other, and strengthen each other's resolve. The echo chamber is a love fest; social media can feel like a cheerleading platform for people's shared

3.3 Echo Chambers and Conspiracy Theories

commitments. An intervention is most effective if it appreciates this fact. One might have plenty of sympathy for the people living there (one might be living there oneself), and respect their assessment of things, but refrain from trusting just any source that they endorse and rejecting any source that they reject. That would be because, while one's heart is with them, it is also with other things, such as the country as a whole, the Earth, humanity, and perhaps most importantly here, the truth.

We have seen that Pascal recommends first conceding that which the other sees *correctly* in the situation. It is correct, I might concede, that politicians are often shady, that we cannot trust everything we read, and that scientists have been wrong about a lot of things before. Surely there *are* people who might profit from widespread belief in climate change, and this should make us somewhat hesitant to accept their word. I have now acknowledged that there is something to the denier's *position* even if not to their conclusion.

The next step is to ask: why is your heart here rather than there? Why is your primary allegiance to this coal country politician? Can you love the same thing but in a different way? Isn't the country, or humanity, as worthy of your allegiance as your favored politicians? Shouldn't we also care deeply about the earth, since we and our descendants must live here? (This is not to mention the most Pascalian thing to say here, which is that the Earth and the sky are God's creation and therefore deserve our reverence.) Perhaps the coal country politician is not as worthy of love and devotion? This has downstream effects on the conspiracy theory. For example, if scientists are so often wrong, why do you think that the minority, endorsed by this politician, who doubt climate change are right? And finally, we might ask: wouldn't it be better to consider the other perspectives, the ones you've been undermining and ignoring, given that they too are in a position to disregard yours?

At the very least, pressing these kinds of considerations, which brought them to their perspective in the first place, brings attention to the fact that the world is ambiguous, matters can be seen in different lights, and we do not always see from all the relevant perspectives. Recognizing ambivalence serves to make one humble, as we've seen, and extremes look less attractive, because they seem inherently parochial and arbitrary. Moreover, one is led by the questions in the previous paragraph to ask oneself: what kind of person am I being? What am

I loyal to and whom do I serve? One can then reconsider how one got to where one is. These reflections are all conducive to resolution, or at least diminishing polarization, or moderation.

There is a point worth repeating and reminding. While we should all recognize the ambiguity of the world and that the heart always influences us one way or another, it is very much not the case that, for a Pascalian, all views are equal, equally supported by evidence, or that all states of the heart are equally good and conducive to correct belief. The state of heart that is best is the one best aligned with reality – the Pascalian is no relativist. The best motivation is the motivation to find the truth, and the only other worthy motivation is one generated by loving that which is objectively worth loving. But most importantly, in matters such as climate change, you should (if you want to believe correctly) love the truth, your motivation should be to figure out whether and how the climate is changing. And only some loves are consistent with that (such as loving the Earth or its creator) while others warp such inquiry (such as loving a person with some economic or political interest in the matter). If your primary concern is to revere and respect nature as the work of God, you are less likely to disregard signs that, for example, some coal country politician is trying to dupe you and helping to pollute the planet.

The ambiguity of the world, even when it comes to such matters of immediate social concern, suggests that in order to see things right, we must put our hearts in the right place.

CHAPTER 4

Desires and Distractions

There is more to your life than what you believe. You also want certain things, you want your life to go (or not to go) this way or that, you want various kinds of things for yourself and others, and you have to make decisions about what desires to pursue and how. Moreover, you feel not just about other things and people but also about yourself. You can feel satisfied, frustrated, happy, desperate, and so on. Pascal's insights go beyond the epistemology and metaphysics that we have explored in Chapters 1–3, and his thoughts about desires, decisions, and the source of our misery are just as worthwhile. Like his epistemological ideas, Pascal's thoughts about our broader lives are ultimately based on Augustinian theology and biblical texts reimagined for modern times. They revolve around the heart, and are aimed at religion. And just as in his epistemology, here we see that, in the process of pursuing his apologetics, Pascal was able to discern and illuminate a lot about our modern condition, even setting the religious element aside.

Pascal's primary aim in this area was to diagnose what is wrong with us in order to motivate a change. But the change is not so straightforward, because what is wrong with us is not so simple. At the root of the problem, as before, is the state of our hearts in the fallen condition. In this condition we love and want the wrong things: we love ourselves and want worldly things. Because we love and want the wrong things, we are deeply miserable even if we get what we want. We grasp, at some level, this hidden frustration – hidden because if all one reflects on is what one currently wants, then one might get the impression that one is doing quite well as long as one gets what one wants. In order to avoid the devastating conclusion that we are unsatisfied even when we get what we want and we pursue what we think matters, and in order to avoid facing our mortality and the sense that we are capable of greatness and are failing to live up to it, we distract ourselves. These distractions lead to myriad pathologies, including self-deception and deception of others, and even the construction of false identities and fake personas. As we will see, Pascal's ideas here read as if they were written for the TikTok age.

The observation that many of us lead what amounts to a lie, that we want the wrong things and therefore are miserable even when successful, is inspired by Ecclesiastes, a book of Scripture that had an enormous impact on Pascal.[1] This book of the Bible is said to have been authored by King Solomon, a sort of address to his people about life. "All is vanity" it is written in Chapter 1 of Ecclesiastes, in the King James version – the Hebrew, in my understanding, is a little different, and "futility" is a common alternative English translation; "fleeting breath" is the preferred translation among some experts. Leaving the subtleties of translation aside, the King James translation continues: "All things are full of labour; man cannot utter it: the eye is not satisfied with seeing, nor the ear filled with hearing" (1:8). We struggle for this or that, but it's meaningless and we are never satisfied. We grasp this, somehow, but try to ignore it. There is nothing new under the sun, Solomon preaches, and everything repeats regardless of what we do in our expendable and replaceable lives. We all are mortal, just like the beasts, and we leave as we came, naked and alone. Whatever we accomplish will be gone, or enjoyed by others who are sometimes less deserving, and at any rate it will all perish and then perhaps be repeated. It is hard to see what point there is, then, to what we do in the few intervening years between birth and death. At one point Solomon suggests it is better never to have been born at all (6:3–6). The challenge is to see what to do about this, aside from despair.

Today, a Pascalian diagnosis of what we do *wrong* in reaction to the apparent futility of life goes something like this. When we constantly check our phones, post on social media, and essentially construct an identity for others to see (something that Pascal was sensitive to long before TikTok and Instagram, as he was writing even before Friendster

---

[1] See Sellier Philippe (2010). Salomon de Tultie: l'ombre portée par l'Ecclésiastes dans les Pensées. Port-Royal et la littérature: Pascal, pp. 221–237, and Moriarty (2020) p. 228.

and Myspace), we are drawing attention away from what is wrong with us, avoiding the full realization that we and our efforts amount to nothing and will soon end. Recall that, for Pascal, we are but delicate reeds. We are delicate in the sense of being mortal – Pascal will remind us, below, that any moment death comes – but we are also delicate in the sense of being often too weak to confront our fundamental problems.

Why are we like this? Much of Pascal's reflection on our miserable condition can be aptly put under this heading: the misery of man without God. For Pascal, the human condition is defined by the Fall. We are God's creation, made in His image, but we have turned our backs on Him, collectively, since our expulsion from the garden of Eden. As a result, we are thoroughly corrupt, can see nothing past our mortality as we live essentially as beasts, and are rotten to the core – the worm at the core of the human condition, William James once wrote, is our knowledge of our mortality – and this corruption operates in the heart. Our sorry state is explained by our concupiscence. Pascal applies this theology to our actual situation, and in doing so identifies real problems, and uses these incisive descriptions of what ails us to motivate a change of heart, or an attempt to change our fundamental orientation to the world. As in his epistemology, we cannot go it alone, we will need outside help from beyond ourselves as individuals. This can be appreciated even before deciding on what the external anchor is (perhaps it need not be God, as I will suggest in Chapter 6). What can be shown by reason, Pascal thinks, is that there is something very much wrong with us, and that it is very much worth our *trying* to reach out beyond ourselves for this change. It is the reasonable thing for a post-Fall human to do.

Before proceeding, a preliminary objection must be aired. In this chapter, we will see plenty of convincing descriptions of how corrupt and miserable we are. But this is a rather one-sided view to have about us. The immediate reply, on behalf of Pascal, is that he *also* says we are capable of greatness, and sometimes we manage to achieve it. When we do, it is thanks to religion. But the objection can be pressed further: even *atheists* who have no religion are not merely corrupt, miserable creatures. There is plenty of good in humankind even in what Pascal considered to be the "fallen" state. Atheists, after all, are capable of incredible acts of selflessness and kindness, not to mention highly evolved and self-aware psychologies. To this, I cannot offer any definitive reply, but nor should I. My aim is not to set the record straight on fallen human nature. Rather, my aim is to motivate reading Pascal today. His observations about the dark side of human nature, at least, are remarkably relatable, even to the atheist who does not consider herself an awful person. Moreover, surely Pascal knew this. He is motivating a change of heart, and for that reason focusing primarily on what is wrong with us when our hearts are in the wrong place. But surely, and some would say with God's grace, we are not *all* bad, even if Pascal insists that the deepest part of us is. Let us grant this point, then, and proceed.

4.1 Our Defective Natures: Don't Follow Your Heart!

We've seen the effect of concupiscence – our fallen state of heart – on our beliefs: we see the world all wrong, missing the most important part of it, the creator, and we believe badly on that basis. But that is not the extent of the damage due to our fallen state. In loving the wrong things, we corrupt our whole selves, not just our beliefs. This makes us miserable, often without even being able to articulate why or how. Since we want the wrong things, even when we get what we want we are still uneasy and unsatisfied. And this is just what Solomon shows again and again in Ecclesiastes: he tries out different ways to live, different things to want; he succeeds, and yet still this is all "vanity," and he is restless. Pascal's variations on this theme are brutal.

Our lives as fallen beings are characterized by "inconstancy, boredom, anxiety" (S58/L24), and this is attributed to the heart:[2] "How hollow and full of garbage is the heart of man" (S171/L139). Many of us might not feel so miserable. This is because we can often enough satisfy our desires, and we are therefore blind to our condition. We are usually self-satisfied in this state, or else we think that if only we can satisfy more of our desires, we will finally be happy.

But the fundamental problem is a pathology of the heart, not a failure to satisfy desire: we don't have the right desires. With the wrong desires you base your actions, aimed at satisfying those wrong desires, on the

---

[2] Readers of nineteenth-century philosophy will probably notice that this diagnosis is echoed in Schopenhauer, and Pascal's solution in some ways resembles Kierkegaard.

4.1 Our Defective Natures: Don't Follow Your Heart

wrong aims. And as Pascal points out repeatedly, the relief of desire satisfaction is short-lived, and we then take on new desires. So real happiness is not the same thing as desire satisfaction.

> Since nature makes us constantly unhappy in every condition, our desires depict for us a happy condition, because they join to the condition in which we are, the pleasures of the condition in which we are not. And if we attained these pleasures, we would not be happy even then, because we would have other desires suitable to this new condition. (S529/L639)

To make things worse, we misdiagnose our problem. We tend to think that if only we were more true to ourselves, we'd be better off, that we should shun external influences on what we want. We think that the key to happiness is to satisfy our truest, most inner desire that defines who we really are. But this is exactly wrong, according to Pascal. This sort of self-love is the root of our problems. There is nothing good about who we truly are in our current state. Pascal's remarks on self-love clash directly with contemporary "self-help" thinking. Don't love yourself, don't try to seek what your true self wants. That is all corruption, and it is what makes you miserable. Only seeking something outside of yourself and beyond the things you want for yourself will save you. It is as if we are caught up in a whirlpool along with the rest of creation, and we reach for objects that are caught with us, as if that will help us rise out of danger. We need instead to reach for that external anchor, outside of the swirling water. This is as true for our desires as it is for our beliefs.

As you read this, you may be thinking that this doesn't apply to you. Your life is not a whirlpool! You feel happy enough. But feeling relatively ok most of the time is not an indication that you are doing ok. From the inside, your secular beliefs may look fine too, because the world looks to confirm, or at any rate it fails to contradict, those beliefs. Similarly, it can feel ok from the inside when your heart generates the wrong desires, even if it also means that you are easily discouraged and depressed. "It takes little to console us because it takes little to distress us" (S77/L43). And this is because we are so thoroughly corrupt and full of ourselves that everything we want is guided by that misguided desire. The world is ambiguous not only in seeming to confirm contrary sets of beliefs but also in seeming to reward or satisfy contrary sets of desires.

4 Desires and Distractions

Part of what makes desire satisfaction feel sufficient for happiness, despite the fact that we have the wrong desires and are never satisfied, is our false sense of importance and self-esteem. Along with the love of oneself comes a feeling of contentment: you can do no wrong as long as you are true to yourself, especially in deciding what you want. Just follow your heart, they say. But that makes sense only if you're satisfied with the state of your heart. To have in your heart self-love means that your fundamental orientation – the way you come to the world, what you want out of it, and what you want to see in it – orbits around the pull of yourself. This leads not only to misery but also dishonesty. Misery because we are, without God, flawed and corrupted, and dishonesty because of the lengths we go to avoid seeing that our true fallen hearts are corrupt, or seeing our various imperfections. This motivates us to hate the truth and build up a fiction to hide it from others (for vanity) and ourselves (for self-love). Such a person is just a disguise, a persona, and all our relationships are built on this lie.

> The nature of self-love and of this human self is to love only self and to consider only self. But what will it do? It cannot prevent this object it loves from being full of faults and wretchedness. It wants to be great, and sees itself small; it wants to be happy, and sees itself wretched; it wants to be perfect, and sees itself full of imperfections; it wants to be the object of men's love and esteem, and it sees that its defects deserve only their dislike and contempt. This embarrassment in which it finds itself produces in it the most unrighteous and criminal passion imaginable, for it conceives a mortal hatred against this truth admonishing it and convincing it of its faults. It wants to annihilate this truth, but, unable to destroy it in its essence, it destroys it as far as possible in its own knowledge and in that of others; that is to say, it devotes every care to hiding its faults both from others and from itself, and it cannot endure that others should point them out or notice them.
> . . .
> Man is, therefore, only disguise, falsehood, and hypocrisy, both in himself and with regard to others. He does not want to be told the truth. He avoids telling it to others. And all these dispositions, so far removed from justice and reason, have a natural root in his heart. (S743/L978)

4.1 Our Defective Natures: Don't Follow Your Heart

Self-love leads not only to a rejection of truth and blindness to our real condition but also to an overwhelming pursuit of fame and external validation:

> We are so presumptuous that we would like to be known throughout the world, even by people who will come when we are no more. And we are so vain that the esteem of five or six people close to us pleases and satisfies us. (S152/L120)

This vanity makes us not only miserable but also foolish, and we are led to focus on cultivating admirers, thereby making ourselves and our happiness (such as it is) beholden to others whose hearts are as defective and self-obsessed as our own.

The idea that we are so fake, or that we fabricate an identity for the purpose of admiration by others, was incredibly prescient in anticipating our natural attraction to social media, where we show off to others how we travel, cook, dress, make music, or pursue hobbies, all for display:

> Curiosity is most often only vanity. We want to know something simply to talk about it. In other words, we would not travel the sea in order to say nothing about it, just for the pleasure of seeing without the hope of ever communicating anything of it. (S112/L78)

This fragment could've been written about TikTok or Instagram today:

> We are not satisfied with the life we have in ourselves and in our own being: we want to live an imaginary life in the minds of others, and for this purpose we endeavor to make an impression. We labor constantly to embellish and preserve this imaginary being, and neglect the real one. And if we are calm, or generous, or faithful, we are eager to make it known, so as to attach these virtues to our other being, and would rather separate them from ourselves to unite them with the other. We would willingly be cowards to acquire the reputation for being brave. This is a great sign of our own being's nothingness, of not being satisfied with the one without the other, and of renouncing the one for the other! For whoever would not die to save his honor would be infamous. (S653/L806)

All of this suggests that one of the chief motivators of human life is vanity, the most direct result of our excessive self-love:

> Vanity is so anchored in the human heart that a soldier, a camp servant, a cook, a dockhand brags and wants to have his admirers, and even

philosophers want them; and those who write in opposition want to have the glory of having written well; and those who read them want the glory of having read them; and I writing this have perhaps this desire, and perhaps those who will read it. (S520/L627)

Pride takes such natural hold of us in the midst of our miseries, errors, etc., that we even lose our lives gladly, provided people talk about it. (S521/L628)

It is not only the foot soldiers who would sacrifice themselves that are miserable. None of us can ever be happy, not even rulers and kings like Solomon, unless we renounce ourselves and love God instead (S181/L 148). But still it is important to consider rulers and kings, because they show that the lust for fame causes us not only to give ourselves and our own desires premium treatment, it also often leads us to subjugate others as well (S494/L 597).

The remarkably dark thing about Pascal's assessment of our fallen natures (aside from its accuracy) is that we are incapable of helping ourselves out of it. Just as reason and experience alone cannot create knowledge or right belief, so they and the natural disposition of our hearts cannot create the right desires, a good life or happiness. We are, by default, miserable creatures, just as we are by default quite ignorant about the nature of the world. We instead must somehow renounce ourselves (S253/L270), disown our own desires, and seek a change in order to come to love God instead (S237/L205). The only hope is to become something else, something that is not so unjustly self-centered. This is to become a human with a different nature, not the fallen-human nature.

So goes life as most of us know it, a life of concupiscence. You treat the world as if it is for you, you try to enslave it and others whether you recognize this or not. This is how you engage with the world, by grasping at it. In a sense, *self*-improvement is impossible. You need to become a new self, get a new heart. The crucial thing in accomplishing this transformation is to decide to try to get help from without, not from within.

So far, we have focused on the corruption of our natures by tracing the consequences of wanting the wrong things. But, as in Ecclesiastes, there is another, major source of misery in the post-Fall, secular life, and that is our mortality and, worse, our knowledge of it.

For Pascal as for many philosophers through the ages, a key feature of the human condition is that it is limited, finite. We are mortal; we each will die. The way we think about our mortality, and even how far away we regard death, has a profound effect not only on how we think about life but also on how we live it.

> We must live differently in the world, depending on these different assumptions:
> Whether we could always exist in it.
> Whether it is certain we will not exist in it for long and uncertain if we will exist in it for one hour.
> This last assumption is ours. (S187/L154)

Pascal wanted us to think of life as if it could end very soon, perhaps because this boils down our situation to its fundamentals, and perhaps it will reveal the rot in our hearts and our misplaced desires and bring to light what matters most. Death is something we typically try to ignore by distracting ourselves with pleasures and other pursuits. We are living in a constant state of denial of death.[3] But what kind of misery is this, to spend your short and limited time alive in denial of reality? It turns out that, tragically, these distractions from the truth only lead to more misery new further problems.

4.2 Unhappiness Leads to Distraction

We are fundamentally unhappy, since we want the wrong things. But we can distract ourselves from staring that fact in the face, by diverting our attention, and our will, elsewhere and anywhere other than on the seemingly insurmountable task of wanting something other than what we currently want. This strategy of diversion has a number of features that will feel familiar today. The first and most important is that it prevents many of us from finding the solution, which is to seek a state of heart that is different from our current one, or to try to change our current orientation.

---

[3] Centuries later, a classic book of psychoanalytic theory takes up this idea: Becker, Ernest (1973). The denial of death. New York: Free Press.

> Wretchedness. The only thing that consoles us for our miseries is diversion, and yet this is the greatest of our miseries. For it is mainly what prevents us from thinking about ourselves, leading us imperceptibly to our ruin. Without it we would be bored, and this boredom would drive us to seek a more solid means of escape. But diversion amuses us and guides us imperceptibly to death. (S33/L414)

We can see here one major source of Pascal's aversion to "pleasures," which often comes off as excessive moralizing. Today we can think of nothing more pure and good than a parent's wholesome love of her child. But for Pascal, indulging even this kind of relationship, if we derive pleasure from it that diverts our attention from the condition of our hearts or from the only thing that can redeem it (God), is an obstacle to be surmounted. Diversion prevents us from the moral and existential imperative to *think well* – recall that, for Pascal, this means thinking about your actual situation in the world. Even the love of a child can easily serve to anchor you more deeply in this world, in creation, rather than contemplate what is beyond it, its creator.

But if our task is to find insights that we can benefit from today in Pascal, we need not focus on the most extreme implications of his principles. It is not hard to recognize that seeking distractions can be an obstacle to thinking well, even when those distractions feel righteous and bring pleasure. Those who don't think well (which is most of us) fail to infer from their distractions that they are not *really* happy. This is despite the fact that the inference is simple and staring us in the face:

> If our condition were truly happy, we would not need to divert ourselves from thinking about it. (S104/L70)

Another consequence of diverting ourselves is that we often don't live in the present reality around us, but instead live in a sort of imaginary world that is always aimed at some future satisfaction (S653/L806). This explains scrolling through Instagram at people performing fitness routines, incredible feats, or traveling the world, and transporting yourself into a fictional scenario in which *you will do that, that will be your life.*

This element of Pascal's account of our fallen condition is reminiscent of a classic Buddhist critique of the "monkey mind," going from one bright shiny thought to the next, but seldom focusing attention on the present. And it is prescient of today's often heard advice to be "mindful" and "live in the moment." Pascal's remarks on this are worth careful consideration in light of these trends, because he presents our lack of presence in an altogether different light. It is bad to never be present and attend to reality, not because the present is so great, not because we are thereby being inauthentic to our true selves, but because diversion helps us avoid the reality that we *are* miserable, we need to fully appreciate how unacceptable our current, real state is, in order to make the effort to change.

> We never keep to the present time. We anticipate the future as too slow in coming, almost to hurry it up, or we remember the past, to stop it as having gone too fast. So imprudent are we that we wander about in times that are not ours and do not think of the one that belongs to us, and so vain are we that we dream of those that are nothing and let slip away without reflection the one that exists. It is that the present is usually painful. We hide it from our sight because it distresses us; and, if it is agreeable, we regret seeing it slip away. We try to support it with the future and think of arranging things we cannot control, for a time we have no certainty of reaching.
>
> Examine your thoughts, and you will find them wholly occupied with the past or the future. We almost never think of the present, and if we do so, it is only to shed light on our plans for the future. The present is never our end. The past and the present are our means; only the future is our end. So, we never live, but hope to live, and, as we are always planning to be happy, it is inevitable we should never be so. (S80/L47)

Pascal's reflections here are so similar, even if at cross-purpose, to discussions of mindfulness in our day that he even remarks on the difficulty of directing attention to the present, as an impediment to reason. Our wandering mind, since it is so uneasy with its current state, prevents us from thinking well:

> The mind of this supreme judge of the world is not so independent that it is not liable to be disturbed by the first noise in its vicinity. The din of a cannon is not necessary to hinder its thoughts; it needs only the creaking of a vane or pulley. Do not be surprised if right now it does not reason well: a fly is buzzing in its ears.
>
> This is enough to render it incapable of good reflection. If you wish it to be able to reach the truth, chase away the animal holding its reason in check and disturbing that powerful intellect, ruler of towns and kingdoms. (S81/L48)

The constant need for and intrusion of distractions amounts to a standing repulsion to the present moment, resulting from our dim awareness of our actual misery. As he puts it, powerfully and in one of the more memorable passages of the *Pensées*, "man's unhappiness arises from one thing alone: that he cannot remain quietly in his room" (S168/L136). This should resonate with us today, and seems experimentally confirmed. For example, Harvard's "happiness" expert Daniel Gilbert recently conducted an experiment in which subjects apparently preferred giving themselves painful electric shocks to avoid sitting quietly alone with their own thoughts![4]

This inability to be present, let alone contented in the present moment, plagues others besides ordinary people who have to suffer pedestrian annoyances. It applies to kings, too, like Solomon. A long fragment, S168/L136, is a masterful description of our meandering and unsatisfiable mind and will, and well worth a careful read for today's self-help audience. In this short excerpt, Pascal writes that all fallen humans have

> sought only a violent and vigorous occupation that turned them away from thinking about themselves, and therefore chose an alluring object to charm and strongly attract them ... it is the hunt and not the kill they seek ... without diversion there is no joy. With diversion there is no sadness. (S168/L136)

Diversions effectively leads us into imaginary lives (S653/L 806), as we attempt to find happiness by avoiding thinking about what might actually make us happy (S166/L133).

We spend endless hours on social media, doom scrolling, pornography (as it is written in Ecclesiastes, Chapter 2, "I refused my eyes no pleasure"), or whatever other contemporary attention magnet we've accustomed ourselves to. How many times have you checked your phone since you started reading this chapter? And many of those who do focus on themselves too often, for Pascal's view anyway, do it for self-love or to manifest themselves more authentically. This is of course

---

[4] Wilson, Timothy, Reinhard, David, Westgate, Erin, et al. (2014). Just think: The challenges of the disengaged mind. *Science* 345 (6192): 75–77.

exactly the wrong approach for a human whose fallen nature needs to be fundamentally changed, not nurtured and expressed.

All of this raises the question: if not diversion, then what is the proper response to our miserable condition? How should we deal with our perpetual dissatisfaction, and with our inability to place ourselves objectively in the right order of the universe? Here Pascal describes a rejection of the usual path:

> When I see man's blindness and wretchedness, when I consider the whole silent universe and man left to himself without light, as though lost in this corner of the universe, not knowing who put him there, what he has come to do, what will become of him at death, incapable of any understanding, I become frightened, like someone brought in his sleep to a frightening desert island who wakes up with no knowledge or means of escape. And then I marvel that we do not fall into despair in so wretched a state. I see other people around me of a similar nature. I ask them whether they are better informed than I am.
>
> They tell me they are not. Then these wretched lost souls look around and see some pleasant objects to which they give themselves and become attached. As for me, I have not been able to become attached, and, considering how much more likely it is that there is something other than what I see, I have sought out whether this God has not left some sign of himself. (S229/L198)

Clearly, the right move for Pascal is to seek God: that external anchor that will determine our significance, set us free from our self-love and, we hope, from our corrupted condition. It remains an open question for us, to be addressed in Chapter 6, whether anything else besides Pascal's God can serve as this external anchor.

4.3 Another Confirmation of the Fall

Do not despair! There is a silver lining, which is that we are capable of greatness. The source of all this trouble is concupiscence. Just as concupiscence warps belief and blinds us, it also warps our wills and makes us miserable. But though our cognitive faculties are insufficient, on their own, to change this, they *are* sufficient for understanding that this is happening, if we "think well" enough. We can know that we must try to love the right thing, and then we would not need to build fictional lives around distractions; we could live in the light of day and face ourselves.

That it is within us to realize this is perhaps the most significant and remarkable thing about us, for Pascal. There are a number of features of this knowledge emphasized by Pascal and worth considering.

To begin with, the corruption of your heart, which is incompatible with the good life, is knowable because you sense your potential for greatness. That is, it is only because you could be great (and we were great, before the Fall), that you could be corrupted, and can conceive of your heart as corrupted. The fallen human is miserable in the way that only a being who once was great, or is capable of greatness, can be. Ours is *"the wretchedness of a great lord, the wretchedness of a deposed king"* (S148/L116). So our corruption confirms the Fall, just as hiddenness does.

> For myself, I confess that, as soon as the Christian religion reveals the principle that human nature is corrupt and fallen from God, it opens one's eyes to see everywhere the mark of this truth: for nature is such that it points everywhere to a lost God, both within and outside man.
>
> And a corrupt nature. (S708/L471)
>
> After having perceived all of man's nature, for a religion to be true, it must have known our nature. It must have known its greatness and smallness, and the reason for both. What religion but Christianity has known this? (S248/L215)

Our hearts, on Pascal's view, contain within them a taste of a love of God, or at least an echo of a taste. Enough to make the corruption of our hearts pale in comparison. On this point again Pascal seems to have been influenced by Ecclesiastes: "God has set eternity into the heart of mankind" (3:11) – Pascal mentions Solomon in the context of our fallen natures (e.g. S22/L403) and makes some remarks similar to this (S471/L64). The point for us is that the Fall can explain not only that we are corrupt and capable of greatness but also why and how we can feel this: God has placed an idea of our greatness, which is to say a feel for loving God, in our hearts.

It is also in realizing our wretchedness that we manifest our dignity and superiority to the rest of nature. This is to "think well." Thinking

4.3 Another Confirmation of the Fall

well about our hearts amounts to knowing that our natures have twisted our hearts:

> Man's greatness lies in his knowing himself to be wretched. A tree does not know itself to be wretched . . . be. (S146/L114)

What Pascal makes of our defective natures, then, is completely bound up in his theology. To think well is to realize your faults while realizing that you are capable of greatness, and this uniquely confirms the Fall. But even setting the Fall aside (which Pascal would never want to do), the idea that our defects confirm a certain worldview is instructive in a more general way. The real conditions of your existence, down to your very heart and soul, should be accounted for in your worldview. Pascal's ruminations about God or the nature of reality are not abstract metaphysical musings, they are not detached from human life. Instead, they are rooted in the vulgar realities of actual life. Sure, it is possible that the universe is governed by a Deist God, or maybe several of them. But this doesn't predict our wretchedness, and nor does it provide what we feel to be a realistic way out. Sure, we may just be animals evolved inside of a heartless mechanism of a universe. But that doesn't explain why we *feel* we could be great, and why we are so damaged in a way that the rest of nature is not, because we realize we have let ourselves down, we fail to meet our own standards. The secular, naturalist worldview might be *consistent* with our condition. But it doesn't explain it at its core as the Fall does. For Pascal, this is a disadvantage to the view, because alongside theoretical virtues like simplicity and elegance, Pascal emphasized the need to account for and diagnose our very real and present misery, and to explain the glimpse of redemption whose spark, he thought, we all feel even if dimly. The attempt to understand reality, done Pascal's way, must engage our inner life as it concretely exists in day-to-day reality.

What our corruption shows, at any rate, is that we should consider a remedy to our misery. Insofar as only Christianity makes sense of our sad condition, we should turn to Christianity for its recommendation. If we can just manage to change what's in our hearts, the source of our misery, we can be great. We are at this point thinking strategically about Christianity: what is best for me, for my condition, to feel and therefore believe? We have entered the territory of Pascal's famous wager.

CHAPTER 5

Wager with All Your Heart

"Your nature has two things to avoid, error and wretchedness," wrote Pascal in by far his most famous and widely discussed text, S680/L418. In that sentence he sets up a powerful, controversial idea: we aim at the truth, but not only the truth. This, I think, has been greatly misunderstood. The fragment, lengthy compared to most of the others in the *Pensées* but short compared to almost any philosophical text that has had this much influence and impact, is often referred to as "Pascal's wager," but Pascal entitled it *"infini rien"* or "Infinity nothingness."[1] That infinity is in the title is significant because, as we will see, one of the main original contributions of Pascal here is to show how infinite quantities should affect our assessment of potential consequences of actions. We can understand it as part of the pattern established throughout this book, of Pascal's fascination with how to navigate infinite spaces despite our inability to discover our own measure within them (see, for example, Chapter 1, Section 1.3).

There is an enormous literature – literary, artistic, philosophical, technical, even mathematical – on Pascal's wager. I will not sum up this literature here.[2] Instead, I will explain *infini rien* as it fits into Pascal's texts and thoughts. That is, I will explain this remarkable fragment as what it is: part of the *Pensées* and in the Pascalian framework established in the previous chapters. Scholars often sequester this

---

[1] This is Roger Ariew's translation of the title, though not all translators agree. Some translate it more directly, as "infinite nothing." It seems to me the latter, though more direct, is severely misleading, so I will follow Ariew.
[2] For this, see Hajek & Jackson's *contribution to A Companion to Pascal*, ibid. (forthcoming), which focuses on the probabilistic literature and on infinite quantities in the wager.

fragment not only from the rest of Pascal but also from history in general.[3] This may lead to some fascinating ideas of great interest today. But the aim of this book is to offer reasons to read and think about Pascal's texts, not piece by piece, but as a whole, and the method is to recover from Pascal an overall picture of ourselves and the world that resonates or inspires or is in some other way productively striking for us today. So, the aim in this chapter is to integrate the so-called wager into the rest of a Pascalian view.

To begin, though, I will briefly describe the way that the so-called wager is usually thought of and taught in introduction to philosophy and philosophy of religion classes today. This will serve as a contrast to the project we've been developing. I put it in a text box to make clear that, though this is the argument and objections that we have inherited from Pascal, I do not think it is his argument, and therefore the standard objections don't apply.

> **"Pascal's Wager" as usually described, and standard objections to it:**
>
> The proofs for God's existence are not convincing, and neither are the proofs for God's nonexistence. So, it may as well be 50–50 whether God exists. If you don't believe in God, you stand to lose a lot: if God exists, you are in for a big loss, at the very least missing out on a great reward. If God doesn't exist, then although you were in some sense right to refrain from believing in God, this doesn't amount to a huge advantage, you still lived and died, and face the same Godless death either way.
>
> So, if you don't believe in God, there's effectively 50 percent chance of an enormous loss (whatever the downside is for failing to believe in a God that exists, perhaps even hell!), and a 50 percent chance of a negligible, if any, gain.
>
> Now suppose instead that you do believe in God. If God exists, you stand to gain *infinite* reward in the hereafter, since God rewards believers. If God doesn't exist, you don't stand to lose much. In fact maybe you still gained a little: you lived devoid of existential angst, since you believed in your divine destiny, and perhaps you even reigned in some of your more corrosive desires and excesses due to your religious belief. Wholesome fun is good fun.

[3] See Ryan, John K. (1945). The argument of the wager in Pascal and others. *New Scholasticism* 19 (3): 233–250 on other versions of the wager, and Roger Ariew's *contribution to A Companion to Pascal*, ibid. on the wager in light of the apologetics of his day.

> (cont.)
>
> So, if you believe in God, there's effectively a 50 percent chance of an infinite reward, and a 50 percent chance of negligible gain, at any rate not much loss.
>
> If you are deciding whether it's better to believe or not believe, you are effectively deciding which bet is better, which coin to flip: take a 50 percent chance on an infinite gain, or 50 percent chance on an enormous loss. Obviously you should choose the former: you should believe! Of course, it is impossible to just decide to believe something. So, seeing that believing in God is advantageous to you – it is the dominant strategy, as game theorists say – you should try to get yourself to believe. Hang out with believers, don't read the atheist literature, go to Church, and so on. Hopefully, in living like a believer, you will eventually come to believe it and reap the potential rewards: 50 percent chance of infinite gain. Certainly this is better than the alternative bet!
>
> There are a number of classic objections to this argument. Two are particularly pressing. The first is that, if we don't know anything about God (even that he exists), how do we know that he rewards believers (let alone punishes or withholds from nonbelievers)? The second is that this seems to be an argument for believing something for the wrong reasons. There are effectively two parts to this objection. First, if God knew that you tried to believe in Him only for your advantage, why would he reward that? It's selfish and insincere, and would never fool God. And second, in trying to get yourself to believe something that you have no evidence for, you are embarking on a quintessentially irrational endeavor to cultivate self-deception, to believe for the wrong reason. So, this cannot be rational.

I hope that I have, with that box, scratched your itch to have this material represented in the book. But now that the itch is scratched, let it be out of our system, because in important ways it was never part of Pascal's system, and we can return to the account of Pascal we have been developing. We have tracked Pascal's overall view, beginning in Chapter 1 with the limitations of reason, that we are incapable of knowing our measure or place in reality by reason alone, continuing in Chapters 2 and 3 with an account of the heart and what this means for how the world appears, and then in Chapter 4 about how pathologies of the heart afflicting all fallen humans make our lives miserable. We saw at the end of Chapter 4 that we can *know* that our hearts are in the wrong place, and that while this is a source of weakness and misery, we also can feel that we are capable of greatness. We have only to overcome this fallen state of heart. This is, as it should be, our point of departure for S680/L518, *infini rien*. We will see that its purpose is to change our heart, or our passions, which are the only things that stand in the way of belief aside from the lack of God's grace. And this is an instance of the general point that reason vastly underdetermines what we can believe. It is our hearts that establish the framework within which reasons for belief arise.

If your heart gets changed in the right way, this will affect not only what you believe but also, as we saw earlier, what reasons you have for believing and willing. The result is a new, *rational* set of beliefs and preferences, at least insofar as rationality is a matter of basing beliefs on the available evidence. However, getting to that state is a conversion, not a straightforward rational process, because reasons themselves change when the heart changes. Is your newfound state, brought about by a non-rational conversion, an instance of self-deception because it was guided by a decision about what would be better for you? As we will see, it need not be.[4] But some versions of this kind of process – wanting a belief and positioning oneself in the hope of achieving that belief – do seem irrational or even pathological. It is of great importance, not only for Pascalian philosophy but also for us all today, to figure out the difference. It can sometimes matter how one came to form a belief, and even how one came to have the reasons for belief that one has. This can matter in a way that undermines any claim to its rationality. Such "genealogical" worries are as relevant today as ever.

5.1 Motivating a Change of Heart

At the end of Chapter 4, we arrived at a motivation to try to change one's heart. Here is how Pascal puts it:

> After having shown the lowliness and greatness of man.[5] Let man judge his worth now. Let him love himself, for there is in him a nature capable of good; but let him not, on that account, love the lowliness in him. Let him despise himself, because this capacity is empty; but let him not, on

---

[4] For a discussion among similar lines, see the end of Davidson, Donald (2004). Paradoxes of irrationality. In *Problems of Rationality*. New York: Oxford University Press. pp. 169–187.
[5] Here Pascal signals where, logically, the following thought would fit within his apology for the Christian religion.

that account, despise this natural capacity. Let him hate himself; let him love himself. He has in himself the capacity for knowing truth and being happy, but he possesses no truth, either constant or satisfactory. I would then arouse in man the desire to find the truth; to be ready, free from passions, to follow it where he may find it, knowing how much his knowledge is obscured by the passions. I would want him to hate his concupiscence, which is self-determined, so that it may not blind him in making his choice, nor stop him when he has chosen. (S1S1/L119)

Pascal is advocating a sort of reset. Our concupiscence corrupts and blinds us, it warps our inquiry, and we can know that it does so (by thinking well). So we should want to change our hearts full of concupiscence and instead cultivate a "desire to find the truth." In order to change, we must somehow quiet the passions generated by our concupiscence that obscure the path to truth. The key concepts here are *passions* and *choice*, not belief.

In this light, we can see that what has been motivated by much of the rest of the *Pensées* is a change of heart, not merely the production of a belief. We saw above that belief or faith which is based on any consideration of human reason is not only fleeting and weak, it is "useless for salvation" (S142/L110). It would be odd, then, if Pascal thought that believing or having faith for strategic or practical reasons, for example to become less miserable or for potential infinite reward, is any more useful for salvation. So if "the wager" is supposed to generate belief, how could Pascal think that it generates a useful belief? The aim, clearly, is not really belief but to motivate a change of heart.

We have seen that the heart, as one's fundamental affective orientation, determines one's will, one's passions, and derivatively constrains what one can believe. And we have seen that no matter how one sees things, one always sees things *from* the perspective of one's orientation. That is, all cognitions and decisions take place within the framework set by the heart. So the motivation for a change of heart is not a motivation to somehow influence your passions so that your choices and beliefs are no longer pristine and uninfluenced. *There is no such thing as an uninfluenced cognition or decision* because these are always constrained and guided by the heart. Concupiscence blinds and warps us; the nonbeliever is not in some unadulterated, purely rational state. The only question is *how or by what* should my cognition be influenced? By

5.1 *Motivating a Change of Heart*

default, as a fallen human, it is influenced by concupiscence, by self-love. If Pascal is going to talk a fallen human into changing their heart, he's going to have to appeal to their current heart-state, which is oriented toward self-interest.

To establish that it is indeed our passions that determine our beliefs and choices, even in our fallen state, Pascal shows that what we are willing to believe is always subject to the passions aroused by our practical situation. This is of course just one instance of the general rule, which we discussed in Chapter 1, that our will is the "primary organ" of belief.

> Anyone with only eight days to live will not discover that the best wager is to believe that all of this is not a stroke of chance. Now, if the passions had no hold on us, eight days and a hundred years would amount to the same thing. ... So that passion can do no harm, let us act as if we had only one week to live. (S358/L326)

The amount of time you have left should make no difference to what you should believe about reality, because it makes no difference to what your evidence is. But, if you think you are about to die, what is at stake – your eternal fate – is made much clearer and more vivid, and this is a matter of the passions. You see in that situation that which should always interest you most, but which is out of sight and heart if your death seems far away. The point here is to emphasize that your passions, your heart, can determine what you are willing to choose and believe, or what you discover to be the best "wager."

So here we are aware that our passions make us miserable, aware that they determine what we believe, and aware that if our passions were different, we'd be less miserable and also could believe differently. It seems we should try to change our passions, then.

But none of the material I just discussed is in "*infini rien*," so why do we even need the "wager?" It seems that even without it we've motivated a change of heart, and a consequent change of belief. One reason we need the wager is that there are some serious problems if we leave it at this. What about those who don't feel so miserable in their current state, who are perfectly self-satisfied? So far we have motivated a change of heart primarily by appealing to the "wretchedness" of our condition, which they don't recognize. This is not a rare case. Previously we noted that if one's desires are usually satisfied, and one manages to distract oneself enough, one might not feel particularly miserable. So their current, self-interested condition might not press them to seek a change, they don't *feel* the need to change. This is not to say that Pascal thought it was *reasonable* or *rational* to be uninterested in a change; he describes in various ways the untenability of their position (S183-190/L150-158). But the only way to make them feel the need to change, as we just saw, is to suggest that they "act as if we had only one week to live." Stir your passions to make vivid that this could all come to an end, even your seemingly reasonable pleasure-seeking and self-satisfaction.

By directing attention to the future and our mortality, Pascal opens the possibility for considering another motivation to change the passions, or to soften the heart to allow God, through grace, to incline it. He is going to appeal to your self-interest, directed at the future, to show you that changing your passions is *still* the right thing to do, even by your own corrupt lights, in the sense that it serves your interests.

5.2 Infinity, Nothingness (or "The Wager")

We have now arrived at the rationale for the so-called wager. This fragment, S680/L418, bears the weight of centuries of commentary and analysis and is a foundation of contemporary probability theory and game theory. Here I will address its key components only within the context of our heart-centric discussion.

Pascal is trying to convince a nonbeliever whose heart is full of self-interest to change; the ultimate goal is a change of heart, not *merely* a belief. But it seems impossible to change a heart so that it *loves* something which one does not believe in. Let's suppose that you are this self-loving nonbeliever. Since you do not yet love God, you do not know God or see things as Godly, and that is because the heart defines the framework within which we see the world as undivine (even if it is sometimes nice). As we saw in Chapter 3, you do not see the sky like David did, as declaring God's glory, even if you see a glorious sky. As Augustine put the problem, "who loves that which he does not know?" (*De Trinitate* 8.4.6).

Because it makes little sense to try to convince you to love something you don't believe in, Pascal must take a circuitous route. Recall – it bears

5.2 Infinity, Nothingness (or "The Wager")

repeated emphasis – that belief without God's grace touching your heart is useless for salvation. So, belief itself is not the end. Instead, Pascal's aim is to make you wish you believed like the faithful do, in order to inspire you to change your heart.

The first notable part of S680/L418 concerns God's justice:

> God's justice must be as vast as his mercy. Now, his justice toward the damned is less vast and should be less shocking to us than his mercy toward the chosen.

It isn't entirely clear – not to me anyway – how to understand these words, and this statement often goes unremarked. But it is plausible to interpret it to mean that God's punishment of the nonbelievers is not as vast (or surprising) as his reward of the believers, or the "chosen." (The latter are called the "chosen" because Pascal's Augustinian or "Jansenist" view is that it is up to God's grace whether your heart is set right, so you cannot take full credit for it.) If this is what he meant, it seems directly relevant to the upcoming wager, because there he will appeal to the infinite degree of reward believers receive if God exists, but does not emphasize (as latter philosophers often do when restating the wager) the vast punishment of nonbelievers.

Having established this apparent asymmetry between the lesser punishment and the infinite reward, Pascal makes a mathematical and epistemological point. The mathematical point is about infinity, that we can know it exists without knowing its nature. Similarly, we *could in principle* know that God exists without knowing God's nature. This is a relief because of course we could never know God's nature, limited and finite beings that we are. So, while we do not – we are assuming for the sake of argument – know whether God exists, we *could* come to know this without knowing His nature. How? Pascal has told us, time and time again, in the *Pensées* as well as the earlier essays, that we can know God by a feeling of the heart, by faith. We can feel God's existence like we feel that this is not all a dream. But to those without this feeling, what could they have to go on? A guess? So here is where things stand:

> We know then the existence and nature of the finite, because we also are finite and have extension.

> We know the existence of the infinite and do not know its nature, because it has extension like us, but not limits like us.
>
> But we do not know either the existence or the nature of God, because he has neither extension nor limits.
>
> ... If there is a God, he is infinitely incomprehensible, since, having neither parts nor limits, he bears no relation to us. We are therefore incapable of knowing either what he is or whether he is. This being so, who will dare undertake to resolve the question? Not we, who bear no relation to him.

So according to Pascal's Christianity itself, we nonbelievers – with concupiscent hearts – cannot know that God exists, nor His nature. His next point is that therefore the lack of available grounds cannot itself be a reason against the religion. You, the nonbeliever, should not expect to see any proof of a religion that says that you will have no proof of it. This is a familiar point from our previous discussions: hiddenness corroborates Christianity. But, he imagines you will say, this "does not excuse those who accept it." What reason is there to believe a religion without any proof, even if it *says* there's no proof?

We can understand this kind of rebuttal: not *every* theory that says there is no proof for itself is believable. The theory that the world is made of undetectable miniature squirrels says it is unprovable (because they are undetectable), but there is no excuse for believing it. The difference, of course, is that the squirrel theory has nothing going for it. That is, nothing specific about the theory is manifest in the world, and things would look just the same if the theory were false. In contrast, we've seen throughout the *Pensées* that Christianity or the Fall has a lot going for it, according to Pascal. It is the only worldview (according to Pascal) that explains the ambiguity in the world and within ourselves, and it is the only religion that is compatible with God being hidden for most people. Therefore, it is worthy at least of consideration, since it is at least suggested to us by what is around us and what is felt in our hearts, at least some of us. To which side should we "incline?" as he puts it here? (Recall that, ultimately, we must ask God to incline our hearts for us, as David asks God to do in the Pslams.) Undetectable squirrels don't make sense of why they are undetectable to some, but not all of us – they are undetectable to all – and nor do they make sense of our intimate experience of corruption, some people's blustering

5.2 Infinity, Nothingness (or "The Wager")

self-satisfaction, nor our feeling that we could be much better, even great. We also don't know too many people, let alone admirable people, who believe in the squirrels.

There are a few key moves that Pascal makes at this point. First, since "reason can determine nothing here," the nonbeliever, or those who think we should believe only when there is sufficient evidence or proof, will be tempted to say that the only right thing to do is to refrain from making a choice either way. However, Pascal says, "you must wager. It is not optional. You are committed."

Why does Pascal say this? Because the choice is whether to believe in God or not to believe in God, and whatever you do, you are in one of those states. This is the choice at hand because it is the potential reward of believing that does all the work in Pascal's argument, and only a believer is rewarded (neither an agnostic nor an atheist are rewarded). This is importantly different from the choice whether to believe that God exists or believe that God doesn't exist, because that is not a wager you must take: you can refrain from believing either way. The choice here, though, is: believe it or don't. This is significant because either choice is *influenced by the heart*, or by the passions. The question then becomes, which passions do you want influencing your choice? If we are thinking about this in terms of our self-interest, the question really is which choice is preferable, and then we can see which passions would facilitate that choice.

> Since you must choose, let us see what is the less profitable option. You have two things to lose, the true and the good; and two things to stake, your reason and your will, your knowledge and your beatitude; and your nature has two things to avoid, error and wretchedness. Since you must necessarily choose, your reason is no more offended by choosing one rather than the other. This settles one point.

What point does this settle and how? The settled point is that if you are looking for the most profitable option – as you are because you are self-interested – you need not weigh the effect of your wager on the true, your reason, or your knowledge, the first item of each pair he lists. And this is because your reason is "no more offended" by believing in God or not believing in God. A contemporary reader might be puzzled by this, and it is a source of some criticism of Pascal. Why should we say that belief is no more "offensive" to reason than nonbelief, when reason is silent on the matter? If we want to match beliefs to evidence – proportion our belief to the evidence, as Hume famously put it – then surely the best match for having no evidence is no belief! But this fundamentally misses a crucial point, one that was not clearly articulated, to my knowledge, until William James' Pascalian classic, *The Will to Believe*.[6] This is potentially an enormously important principle for contemporary epistemologists, and so worth the brief detour.

James' justification for Pascal's move here is that one who values truth (and reason and knowledge are assumed to aim at the truth) has two aims. That is, there are two ways to value truth. One is to avoid error, and the other is to believe important truths. If all you care about was avoiding error, then your task is simple: don't ever believe anything, and you are sure to avoid error! The problem is that you've sacrificed knowledge, or believing important truths. If there can be no way, even in principle, for you to settle a matter on the basis of evidence and proof, then whether you choose to believe or not believe will come down to which of the two aims you value *more*.[7] If you are more concerned with avoiding error, then you should choose not to believe. If you are more concerned with believing important truths, you should choose to believe. Which you are more concerned with is a matter of your passions, it is not a matter of reason, so reason is equally unoffended by either choice. This is because reason itself does not prefer avoiding error over believing truths (or vice versa).

This way of defending Pascal raises a number of questions. Won't believing in something with no evidence or proof lead to more arbitrary and unsupported beliefs that you go on to infer? Isn't the well now poisoned? And how could you really rely on such a belief if you *know* that there is no evidence for it? To these, a number of answers are

---

[6] James, William (1995). *The Will to Believe: And Other Writings from William James*. New York: Image Books. Edited by Trace Murphy.

[7] Following Pascal, James restricted this to only *some* matters, in particular what he called "genuine" options. This closely follows Pascal: the option must be "forced" in the sense that whatever you do you are choosing an option, such as when faced by the choice of whether to believe or not; the option must be "live" in the sense of believable or not absurd like the undetectable squirrels, and Pascal argues, as we've seen, that Christianity is such a live option; and the option must be momentous in the sense of making a significant difference to your current and future life, as Pascal has argued that the matter of God surely is.

5.2 Infinity, Nothingness (or "The Wager")

possible, and we should not get bogged down in all of it. Instead, let us see why these questions don't apply to Pascal's case at hand, the matter of God's existence, within Pascal's own epistemology.

Set aside James' important distinction between the two aims – James deserves a book-length treatment (or several) on his own. A more direct way to investigate why reason, truth, and knowledge are "no more offended by choosing one rather than the other" is to see what happens *after* each choice is made. That is, let us see which is "the more profitable option" from the point of view of reason, truth, and knowledge. How should we asses, given reason's silence on the matter currently, a situation in which we come to believe that there is a God? We cannot assess that this would make our beliefs *less* accurate than they are now, because we have no reason to believe that God doesn't exist. (That is part of the opening assumption of the wager.) So the overall accuracy of our beliefs does not suffer if we add belief in God to it, and the resulting system of belief is just as coherent as it is now. Same, of course, goes for adding the belief that God *doesn't* exist, or keeping any belief either way out of our system. From where we stand now, all these resulting systems are equally accurate, or likely to be accurate, because our reason is silent on the matter of God's existence. Thus, there is no less profit, potentially, in wagering one way or another, with respect to truth, reason, or knowledge. To object that adding a belief is "riskier" than withholding a belief, so that the resulting system is made less accurate by adding belief that God exists (or that God doesn't exist), is to value avoiding error more than believing truth, and it is here that James' point is needed. Accuracy is not *merely* avoiding error.

Moreover, we have seen that once your heart is in the right place and you *do* believe in God, you will see plenty of evidence and reasons for believing – in the world, in your life, in the church, and so on. So your resulting belief, if all goes well and as Pascal predicts, will not only maintain your current level of accuracy but it will also become supported by reasons, which you will be able to access in your future state. (Of course, the same is true if you don't believe, in which case you will see the world in such a way that makes nonbelief seem reasonable.) This, at least, is how things will be for the believer according to Pascal's view from our previous chapters, given the ambiguity of our world. Reason is not only unoffended, it will also actually *support* your choice, either way.

Finally, with all of this background established, we come to the actual bet. We just saw that there were two things you risk in this wager: "knowledge and beatitude," accuracy, and practical gain. With respect to knowledge or accuracy, you don't stand to lose or win anything by wagering either way as far as you can tell. So we move on to the second risk:

> But your beatitude? Let us weigh the gain and the loss in calling heads that God exists. Let us assess the two cases. If you win, you win everything; if you lose, you lose nothing. Wager, then, without hesitation that he exists! "This is wonderful. Yes, I must wager. But perhaps I am wagering too much." Let us see: since there is an equal chance of winning and losing, if there were two lives to win for one, you could still wager. ... But here there is an infinite life of infinite happiness to be won, there is one chance of winning against a finite number of chances of losing, and what you are staking is finite. All bets are off wherever there is an infinity and wherever there is not an infinite number of chances of losing against the chance of winning. There is no time to hesitate; you must give everything.

The particular finite quantities don't matter. If you wager that God exists, you have something infinite to gain (if God exists), and only something finite (if anything) to lose. Whatever there is to lose if you believe in God and there is none – and we will see below that in fact Pascal thinks there is instead something to gain – it is at most finite. This is because those losses are compiled in your one, finite life. This is the familiar point, that the dominant strategy, the best expected utility, comes from wagering on God.

> Thus our proposition is infinitely powerful, when the stakes are finite in a game where the chances of winning and losing are even, and the infinite is to be won.
> This is conclusive and if people are capable of any truth, this is it.

What objection is there left to make? The smart bet is that God exists, since it's about as likely to be true as not, you have infinitely much to gain, and nothing (or at most something finite) to lose. Everything is exactly even except these possible outcomes.

The problem, of course, is that as a self-interested nonbeliever, though you may see the advantage of believing, you cannot simply decide to believe. The best you can do is *try* to believe, and we have seen above that this means trying to see the world a certain way, to put your heart in a certain state. In other words, what the wager motivates is for you to *seek* God, not to decide to believe in God.

5.3 The Benefits of Seeking

The rest of S680/L418 deals with the fact that we cannot simply decide, voluntarily, to believe something once we see some advantage to it. If your heart is hardened against the possibility that God exists, the wager motivates you to soften it. But recall that the wager is forced upon you, since either way you decide on one side (believe) or another (don't believe). Nature, your *fallen* nature, has decided the matter for you:

> "I am forced to wager, and am not free. I have not been released and I am made in such a way that I cannot believe. What, then, would you have me do?" That is true. But at least realize that your inability to believe comes from your passions, since reason brings you to this and yet you cannot believe.

The first step is acknowledging you have a problem. Nature (since the fall) made you such that you cannot believe. It did this through hardening your heart. You cannot, by your own efforts, bring yourself to do the beneficial thing. "It is in vain, O men, that you seek within yourselves the remedy for your miseries. All your enlightenment can only bring you to realize that you will find neither truth nor good within yourselves" (S182/L149). But all is not lost, because you are not alone:

> Work, then, on convincing yourself, not by adding more proofs of God's existence, but by diminishing your passions. You would like to find faith and do not know the way? You would like to be cured of unbelief and ask for the remedies? Learn from those who were bound like you, and who now wager all they have. These are people who know the way you wish to follow, and who are cured of the illness of which you wish to be cured.

That is to say, these people have their hearts in the right place.

Consider an analogy. Suppose you are prone to anger. It is reasonable to suppose that you might learn how to calm yourself better by learning from those who used to be angry but are now always calm. How do they react to things? What do they do instead of getting angry, like you would in that situation? This procedure of looking to those who have been cured is common sense. But how, exactly, do you learn from someone how to love and believe the right things?

> Follow the way by which they began: they acted as if they believed, took holy water, had masses said, etc. This will make you believe naturally and mechanically. "But this is what I am afraid of." And why? What do you have to lose? But to show you that this is the way, this diminishes the passions, which are your great obstacles, etc.

By doing the things believers do, by living the way they live, you might take on the belief "mechanically." This is usually taken to mean that by acting like a believer, you stand a good chance to become a believer. This is presumably because, by living like them, your passions will match theirs. But I don't think Pascal is assuming some sophisticated view about the relation between behavior and belief, as if to believe, let alone love, is to act like a believer (or to act like a lover). That is not why behaving like the faithful makes you believe "naturally and mechanically." Rather, it is the diminished passions that were blocking belief, the undoing of a hardened heart, that makes you take on the belief "mechanically." It is easily observed and well-documented that people tend to believe in the way they are brought up, and similarly to those who surround them. This is the mechanism of natural belief (what Pascal elsewhere calls "custom"). We can think of the passions that need to be diminished as those that lead you to value avoidance of error or belief of truth, or simply those passions that constitute self-love or concupiscence, which make loving God and seeing the world accordingly so difficult.

One reason to resist Pascal's prescription is to think that it is dishonest to act like believers when you don't believe. It is dishonest to go to mass and pretend you're praying when you don't believe anyone hears the prayer. But whether it is dishonest depends on the intent, and what Pascal is suggesting you do would be done in the spirit of seeking, not pretending. You are fishing, not pretending that you possess a fish. Suppose you are lost in the woods, and don't know if anyone can hear you. You doubt it but harbor some hope. Is it dishonest or pretense to yell out, in case someone, miraculously, hears?

That makes sense, perhaps, for someone who is unsure whether God exists, an agnostic. That is one way to lack belief. But what about the

5.3 The Benefits of Seeking

atheist who feels sure there is no God? For the atheist, it is superstitious to think there is any harm done by acting like a believer. Whom would it offend? Whom does it harm? If He is there, you have everything to gain, and if He is not, your prayers and rituals are just more human psychology, more electro-chemical buzzing in one of billions of little bundles of complexity spinning around the Earth, in a far-flung suburb of a mediocre galaxy in a who knows what kind of ocean of galaxies. It's not causing you or anyone pain, and we already established that it does not offend reason. If anything, this would be a sort of focused mindfulness, you get your mind off other, more earthly things. (This is not to say that there is no morality without God, of course. It *does* harm another creature in a comprehensible way if you cause them pain, for example. But you harm no one and nothing by uttering words with the aim of seeking.)

There is a further point – that the prescribed behavior is aimed at more than producing *mere* belief. The real aim is a change of heart that only God can affect. Why didn't Pascal specify this? Pascal is speaking to a nonbeliever, so he will not be appealing to his theology in trying to convince them – remember from Chapter 1, that in the *Art of Persuasion* and elsewhere, Pascal suggests that we take the other's point of view first when trying to convince them. Instead, Pascal had it in mind to put us into the state – ritual, habits and all – where we are inviting God to grant us grace. As we saw in Chapter 2, we cannot achieve a change of heart alone, and nor can we do this by imitating those who are saved. Only God can incline our hearts by grace. Pascal is encouraging you to act like those who were granted grace, as your best shot at being granted grace as well. Your passions are blocking you from finding God, but getting rid of those passions is merely a necessary, not sufficient condition for salvation. He does not say this explicitly, because he is not talking to someone who already believes in divine grace. Instead, he is only appealing to your self-interest:

> Now, what harm will come to you by taking this side? You will be faithful, honest, humble, grateful, generous, a sincere, true friend. Certainly you will not be taken by unhealthy pleasures, by glory and by luxury, but will you not have others?

> I tell you that as a result you will gain in this life, and that, at each step you take on this road, you will see such a great certainty of gain and so much nothingness in what you risk, that you will at last recognize that you have wagered for something certain and infinite, for which you have given nothing.

The wager, then, should be a no-brainer. This is the meaning of the title, Infinity versus nothingness: you stand to gain infinity and lose nothing. In fact, you stand to "lose" only by becoming a very nice person! The infinite gain and the nothing loss brings us to the end of the famous wager.

There is a loose end to address, though. What of the advantage of believing there is no God when there is no God? This constitutes the opportunity cost, as one might put it, in wagering on God. In that case, do you at least gain some advantage for being right? Maybe technically, but not in any meaningful way. For one, you'll never know this and there is no greater perspective – nothing occupies the God's-eye view, nothing observes your life and its place in the universe – if there is no God, so this information about your accuracy is effectively nonexistent. Moreover, if there is no God, then there truly is no measure of humankind or your own existence. As we saw in Chapter 1, all you are left to imagine is that you are lost between the two infinities. What is it, exactly, to "know" your place between two infinities if there is no God? Wagering against God is wagering against there being any answer to this; it is not wagering that you have some other significance not specified by God in the world. For all you believe, you are not only floating lost, you are undefined in size and significance. As Pascal would surely put it, you may as well be nothing, for all you know. How could it matter much that you didn't believe that you were something, if you are nothing? For Pascal, if there is no God, then nothing matters – not from the self-interested perspective of concupiscence anyway. If so, then it doesn't matter that you refrained from believing something false.

5.4 The Objections and Two Appeals to Self-Deception

Time to reconsider the "classic" objections from our text box at the beginning of the chapter, to see why they don't engage well with Pascal's *Infini rien*.

5.4 The Objections and Two Appeals

Consider first the objection that since we cannot know the nature of God, we cannot know whether or not he punishes and rewards us according to our beliefs. This objection misfires on numerous counts. For one, we've ruled out other religions – at least as Pascal understands them. Deism, for example, doesn't account for ambiguity in nature out there in the world (as we saw in Chapter 3) or our miserable inner natures (as we saw in Chapter 4). Paganism doesn't explain why we can't see the gods. Only Christianity is left standing. The broader lesson to take from this is that the sort of wager Pascal is proposing applies only to a limited range of plausible (or "live") possibilities. It does not apply to possibilities that have no basis or confirmation in reality as we experience it. For Pascal, Christianity is the one religion that could be based on the actual conditions of our existence in this world and within ourselves. Moreover, the aim is to cultivate the right set of passions by changing the heart so that God can grant grace. If Christianity is false and some other, indifferent or uninvolved God exists (say), then the wager fails but not much harm is done. Grace won't come, but that is your current situation anyway.

The fact remains, though, that Pascal in the wager motivates this change of heart by appealing to self-interest and with the stated aim of believing something that one currently sees no reason to believe. So the resulting prescription is to do something that might be described as manipulating yourself to be open to some things that you are currently not open to. This may not sit well with today's reader. This is the objection from self-deception.

As noted, Pascal appeals to self-interest because he is addressing someone who is self-interested, so full of concupiscence that he cannot see that the world is God's. But we need not buy into the Fall or his apologetic project to accept this dialectical maneuver. So long as you accept that rational choices can be made on the basis of self-interest, you can accept Pascal's strategy as one aimed to show that a certain course of action is practically speaking reasonable. What is wrong, after all, with trying to improve your situation by wanting to change your heart? You could reasonably wish to be more loving, more sympathetic, more open-minded. You could reasonably wish to love someone.

Imagine, for example, a depressed person who believes that nothing good will come to them in life. There are reasons to support this belief, sadly, but there are also reasons for hope, depending on what aspect of the world we focus on. Certainly, this is possible in Pascal's epistemology, where the heart is "one of the principal organs of belief" because it determines the will to look at a particular aspect of things rather than another. We all know this well: considering a situation when being sad or angry brings into focus a particular aspect of the situation and obscures another. Pascal's move is like offering the depressed person a reason to try to see things differently, to consider other aspects. To pursue the analogy a bit further, the aims being appealed to must be ones that the depressed person already accepts, or else they will never be convincing. In other words, we will never convince this person to try to see things differently by asking them to assume that there is hope when they are certain there is none. Likewise, Pascal tries to appeal only to things the nonbeliever recognizes, namely, things in their own interest.

At this point, a quick reminder about Pascal's epistemology will help. We have seen that reason and experience vastly underdetermine how things might be, in that they are compatible with reality being any number of different ways – even with all of this being one long dream. Recall, from Chapter 1, that the heart of a human is a key ingredient in a human's conception of things and her beliefs. Some contributions of the heart are naturally and fully general to all humans, and these determine the bounds of what is believable to a human. These boundaries include that this waking life puts us into contact with reality, and basic first principles of logic and geometry. They are generated by feelings of the heart, and in conjunction with reason and experience they form a common core of belief for all humans. Holding only that common core fixed, though, there is still a great variety of things that humans can believe, because the heart of a human can vary widely and so produce a variety of different beliefs in conjunction with a variety of experiences and thoughts.

Return now to Pascal's wager. For Pascal, the two main states of the heart that can determine the most important alternative beliefs of a human are concupiscence and faith. The wager is a pragmatic argument for a practical prescription to take action to switch from concupiscence to faith. To resist this on the grounds that it is self-deception is to ignore the fact that it is just as likely, as far as you know, that the affective state resulting in your current situation is corrupting and warping your thoughts as it is that the state Pascal wants you to aim for is corrupting.

5.4 The Objections and Two Appeals

This follows from the inevitability of the heart's influence in every case. It is as if you are entirely blind unless you wear glasses. You can wear concupiscent glasses or faithful glasses. The wager shows that faithful glasses carry advantages for you, potentially infinite in the afterlife and finite but substantial in this life (recall the corruption and misery that comes with concupiscent glasses). Reason or the matter of accuracy alone gives no preference to one over the other. It's just that seeing things through the one leads to misery and very possibly a great (if finite) loss, and the other to happiness and very possibly an infinite gain.

Furthermore, what we see in the world, including its ambiguity and the diversity of human thought, confirms a view which *explains* why you currently wear concupiscent glasses and how they are inferior to faithful glasses, both in the accuracy with which they represent the world and in the way they make you feel and corrupt your will. In fact, on that view the concupiscent glasses are literally a corruption, a degradation of faithful glasses. Pascal is not suggesting you simply drop the current pair of glasses and put on the faithful ones, because he knows you cannot do that. Instead, he is suggesting you try, by being open and taking steps to have someone switch the glasses for you. Why not *try* to invite this change if you have everything to gain and nothing to lose by trying? At least you will then be able to compare the two views. If the Fall is true, you may well come to enjoy the benefits of the faithful glasses. If it is false, no harm done, you won't get faith, but you still enjoy some finite advantages for having tried – trying makes you a nice person.

There is very little here that seems self-deceptive so far from the perspective of the person about to wager. But is there a problem looking back, once you are granted faith by grace after the wager? Suppose that due to being convinced by the wager you live like believers, your heart becomes less hardened, and you have a change of heart. You begin to see things as believers see them, and come to believe in God. But your memory is intact, and you remember this process. Should the memory of how you came to hold the new belief be any cause of concern or doubt about your new belief?[8]

---

[8] This worry is discussed in Garber, Daniel (2009). *What Happens After Pascal's Wager: Living Faith and Rational Belief*. Milwaukee: Marquette University Press, and at the end of White, Roger (2010). You just believe that because . . . .. *Philosophical Perspectives* 24 (1): 573–615.

To be sure, the genealogy, or causal history, of our beliefs can sometimes be cause for doubt. If I learn that I came to believe something as a result of taking a psychoactive drug, or because there were extremely low oxygen levels in the room, or because I have been manipulated since birth, this is a reasonable cause for doubt. In these cases, though, one's consideration of the history of one's belief seems to involve an acknowledgment that *currently* the reasons one has for believing are illusory or weaker than originally thought. Or else, it is at least an acknowledgment that the way one is weighing the reasons is off. But if the genealogy doesn't clearly imply any such thing, it is less clear what the problem is. What makes assessing Pascal's wager so challenging is that it seems different in important ways from a case of, say, mind-altering drugs.

Suppose there is a great biology professor who excels at presenting convincing evidence for evolution. A young person who was raised religious and believes in creationism might enroll in this professor's class and thereby become convinced, on the basis of that good evidence, in evolution. Looking back, the student can see that, had it not been for that professor, she would not be so confident in evolution and perhaps would still believe creationism. Is that *itself* a reason for doubts? It seems not. We can realize that matters of luck or fate led to our possessing good evidence, without this fact necessarily undermining that evidence. That much seems clear.

This is arguably the case in Pascal's wager: you might think that it was good fortune that you ran into Pascal and his wager, just as the student might think it is good fortune that she enrolled in that class. To help bring this out, consider that, before enrolling in class or considering the wager, one can just as well come to realize that one's views on the matter are influenced by one's upbringing anyway. That is, pre-wager and pre-biology class, what one believes is also a contingent matter of what evidence one happened to have access to, and what state of heart one is in.

The case of the wager is one in which you are trying to see if you can get the kind of evidence that believers appreciate. It is not a case in which you are trying to see if you can arrive at a different conclusion on the basis of the evidence you already have. This seems to make all the difference. Trying, for convenience, to change your mind about what to believe given the evidence that you have does seem fishy. For example,

5.4 *The Objections and Two Appeals*

if the student learns in class, not new evidence, but motivations for believing in evolution and ways to downplay the already existing evidence she has against it, and if the student then reconsiders her previously available evidence with the aim (conscious or not) of believing evolution, we have a very different situation. In that case, she is not seeking new evidence, but she is seeking to believe something on the basis of her old evidence.[9] But in Pascal's case this is not so. What we seek after the wager is a new way of looking at things, so that we can come to appreciate aspects of the world we never saw before. That is, we are seeking new evidence.[10]

This response to the charge of self-deception depends, of course, on Pascal's views about the ambiguous world, that one's state of heart determines how one sees things, and this determines the available bases for belief. Recall that part of this view entails that all ways of looking at the world are influenced by one's heart and will, all reasoning is motivated. But this fact raises a more decisive reply to the objection at hand, which is that since self-deception focuses on matters of belief, the objection misunderstands Pascal's strategy.

As noted in the previous subsection, the reason the wager is framed as a matter of belief is that one cannot love what one cannot see. Or, at least, that is a tough sell. Instead, the aim is to open one up to the possibility that God exists, to make them *want* to believe that God exists. This desire, it is hoped, will invite God's grace into the heart and change it. More generally, the wager is supposed to put you in a position to receive something that inspires belief as well as newly appreciated reasons for belief, such as seeing things in a new light, or seeing Godly aspects of things for the first time. Bearing this in mind, is it self-deception to want a change of heart, or to try to get yourself to love something for your own gain? And once you are in love, is the fact that you tried to fall in love for practical, self-interested reasons serve to

---

[9] See Avnur, Yuval & Scott-Kakures, Dion (2015). How irrelevant influences bias belief. *Philosophical Perspectives* 29 (1): 7–39. There, we call this influence "directional," and argue that it is a defeater to a belief's epistemic justification.

[10] Some epistemologists prefer a more coarse-grained notion of evidence, according to which the evidence stays the same even when one sees the world differently or in different aspects. For them, the present point should be put a little differently: one is not trying to believe something new on the basis of how one already interprets the evidence, but rather trying to understand a different way of interpreting the evidence.

undermine that love, the new reasons it generates, and whatever other cognitive states like beliefs are based on it?

Imagine you have just been subject to an arranged marriage, and have never met or even seen the spouse you will have to marry. You complain: how can I live my whole life with (and for) someone I've never met, let alone love! Your grandfather might be wise enough to know that he won't be able to convince you to *love* your future spouse. But he might try to convince you that, at this point, it is in your interest to be open to it, to try. This is for your own good, the good of the family, our collective security, and so on. So now you decide to try to be open to it and to take steps to make this arrangement work, if you can. Maybe try to act toward the spouse in the way that you've seen other, loving couples act. Of course, things still have to be just right: the future spouse must be lovable, must affect you in the right way, must not be abusive, and so on. That part is out of your hands, of course. But let's say that you determine to try to make it work.

As time passes, you marry, you live, you get into it, and you eventually come to love and cherish your spouse. It turns out this wasn't so difficult, your spouse is graceful and lovable. Why do you love your spouse? It would be perfectly believable for you to answer that you love your spouse because your spouse is lovable, because your spouse is worthy of love, and because you just have the feelings and regards that lovers do. The matters that were out of your hands worked out. Now there may come a time when the grandfather reveals to your spouse the kind of considerations he offered you originally to get you to try to get along and fall in love. And this may, we can imagine, make your all too human spouse a bit upset. "So you love me only because it's in your self interest!" the spouse might say. What do you do then? You repent, to some extent: "I know, I wasn't thinking about things in the right way back then." But then you will plead, honestly: "But now I truly love you, you're my one and only, and I've cast away that whole attitude. Had I known how wonderful you are, I would never have resisted!" How could your spouse reasonably stay mad? The situation you were in is different from the present situation. You didn't know this person back then.

So you can come to love someone for originally selfish reasons, and this need not undermine the significance of the love or the reasons it

5.4 The Objections and Two Appeals 129

generates. And we've seen that love can be the key to belief; the beliefs born of this love, which reveals some otherwise hidden aspects of reality, need not be put in doubt. We can also see that God, who by grace puts love in your heart in the first place, shouldn't be expected to resent the reasons for your trying to love God any more than the spouse in the example should remain angry for long. So we have now a response to what in the textbox at the beginning of the chapter was the "first version" of the self-deception objection as well: that God knows how and why you came to your belief, and would not be satisfied with it. To be clear, there are two replies here: first, it is God who put the love in your heart by grace in the first place, so it is odd to predict that He would also view that love negatively; second, God has as little reason to disdain your love as the spouse does in the arranged marriage case.

The analogy with romantic love is not unheard of, nor is it blasphemous: we find such analogies in the Bible, for example in Song of Songs. But it is complicated by the fact that, to the nonbeliever, the issue seems to be belief, while for the believer, who is really a lover first and a believer second, it is about love. That is to say that if someone doesn't believe in God, there is very little sense to telling them that they should try to love God. But Pascal's wager gets us to think in terms of analogies like this. And so we are invited to think of all investigations, and all beliefs, in a similar way, because as we saw in Chapter 2, we are at bottom *feeling* things, we are hearts with a believing-mechanism added on as an afterthought. Pascal's "cordate" view turns out to be indispensable for understanding the wager. And yet most who write about the wager seem to have no clue about it.

The reply above, to the charge of self-deception, is not clear-cut or conclusive. It is just more evidence of how incredibly rich Pascal's ideas can be. The topic of the genealogy of belief is of great interest today, and there is much to be gained by applying a Pascalian perspective to it. However you see things, this is due to the position of your heart, and that position is due to external factors: the Fall, God's grace, or perhaps just evolution and your current culture. Pascal offers us a view of how a choice might be made to affect our epistemological destiny, and a way to choose according to our interest. Such choices are commonplace in life but not in epistemology. They are choices about what to investigate and how far, how to act, whom to discuss things with, and what aspect of things to seek out. And these are all choices affected, not just by reason but also by our hearts.

At this point, however, a problem arises, one which can be addressed by appealing to a different kind of self-deception. If the wager motivates seeking or trying to soften the heart, what should one do if this doesn't work? Not only do some seek and never find but also some who had love of God in their hearts come to lose it. It seems that one might genuinely wish to have faith, but the seeking never works. They miss out on the potential infinite reward, not because they believe in God but God doesn't exist, but because the project of diminishing their passions, or genuinely seeking, never bears fruit. These are the kinds of considerations that make John Schellenberg's atheist argument from Divine Hiddenness, mentioned earlier, so compelling. And if seeking doesn't work, this obviates the whole point of the wager.

Several responses are available. As we've noted, on one version of Pascal's theology, God is not *required* to grant grace by changing the hearts of those who seek. It is an act of grace precisely because it is not required and not automatic. *Some* will enjoy God's grace, and it is worthwhile (according to the wager) to *try* to make this happen for yourself. For how long is it reasonable to try and keep trying? I doubt Pascal thought that there was a precise answer to this. Try as hard and as long as you can, he probably would have said.

Another, perhaps more promising, reply is that our intentions, motives, and desires are not always transparent to us. We are often wrong about what we really want. You might *seem* to yourself to want your marriage to work, for example, when in fact, not quite consciously, you are sabotaging it. The same might be true with seeking God. You might be convinced of the rationality of seeking but be too attached to worldly things to *really* want faith, or to love God more than worldly things. If so, it might well happen that you seem to yourself to try, you do really want to be faithful, but you are not genuinely seeking.

What does it take, exactly, to "genuinely seek?" There are two layers to this rich question. First, we have examples of "tests" of faith in the Bible that suggest that one is required to be willing to sacrifice all, even more than oneself. This is one interpretation of the trial of Abraham, who was required to be willing to sacrifice his beloved son, Isaac. So on one level, only those who are willing to go *very far* can then rightly complain, if they

5.4 The Objections and Two Appeals

aren't granted grace, that God abandoned them or doesn't exist. (Recall the discussion of S681/L427 in Chapter 3, Section 3.1.)

But how plausible is this? The second layer to the current question is whether such demands by God are *justified*. It seems that for some having faith comes naturally and easily. Some seem to be fully and successfully religious (or "saved") without ever having been tested or required to go to extremes to prove worthy of God's grace. Why does God withhold from some and give freely to others? Recall, though, the discussion in Chapter 2, Section 2.4, of our inability to understand divine justice. The very notion that we are in need of grace, that we are fallen because of some primordial sin is itself offensive to our sense of justice. Who are we to say whether God is just in his distribution of justice?

But these responses have an uncomfortable feature: they presuppose the theology which they are trying to motivate. Whether this is a serious dialectical problem for Pascal is a worthy topic, but one which I leave aside. Instead, it is probably better for the Pascalian to lean more heavily on the earlier notion that we are often self-deceived when it comes to what we are actually seeking. Some spend years (and much money) in therapy trying to figure out what ultimate desires lay beneath their life's decisions and habits. Even if we *seem* to ourselves to genuinely seek or want God, we may well not. Since this sort of self-deception remains a possibility, no matter how we understand "genuine" or "sufficient" seeking, it seems Pascalian theology, of the sort required for the wager, cannot be refuted by this objection.

CHAPTER 6

A Secular Pascalian Vision

Making a case for reading Pascal today requires, at least to some extent, recovering philosophical ideas from his project that are not explicitly theological. Otherwise only those interested in religion will find reason to read him. This is in tension, however, with the fact that Pascal wanted us to adopt his Catholic vision of the religion, sacraments, rituals, masses, and all. He had no use for philosophy otherwise – recall that he sets aside "proofs" for God's existence, for example, and considers human morality (and so presumably the study of ethics) to be defective. Even beyond the *Pensées*, many of his texts are meant to support and defend his Augustinian (or "Jansenist") vision of religion. So naturally, in explaining Pascal, I have appealed to his religion and his religious concerns even while trying to show that he is worth reading for everyone, not just potential converts. This final chapter aims to show that Pascal's big picture has a worthwhile version without theological residue. This includes primarily the Fall and the Abrahamic God, which we have seen figure prominently in much of Pascal's thinking throughout the previous chapters. Certainly, a similar process of filtering out non-secular elements has inspired Leibnizian, Spinozan, and Cartesian ideas. We have already seen that there are important, nontheological insights in Pascal. Is it possible to put these insights together into an integrated Pascalian vision without a role for God?

A secular Pascalian view would naturally begin with skepticism about reason. Our reason and experience are incapable, by themselves, of determining very much about reality, from the abstract claims of geometry to our conviction that life is not like one long dream. We do know such things, but not by the operation of our reason and experience alone. It is, instead, the heart that feels, and through its affective connection to things in the world it determines the framework within which reason operates and in which experience is comprehended. The heart is one's fundamental and affective orientation to reality; it is the foundational connection we have with things external to us.

This cordate epistemology – neither empiricist nor rationalist – does not require God. That is one substantive, secular element of Pascalian philosophy, and one that epistemologists today can and should engage with. We are, at bottom, feeling creatures. This is not so implausible, even without the skeptical arguments. In *Descartes' Error*, António Damásio marshals empirical evidence, from an entirely naturalist point of view, to show that our decision-making would be very poor indeed if it was based solely on reason.[1] Instead, the passions (or emotions) contribute greatly to our choices, and there is little sense to make of reason in human life without the passions. It seems, then, that Pascal's heart-centric approach is not only compatible with but also implied by a naturalist view.

Some other implications of the limits of reason can be appreciated nontheologically as well. That we are lost between the two infinities (the infinity big and the infinitely small) is of course a major Pascalian theme. It amounts to a further skepticism about a sort of philosophizing that aims to establish for us a level of significance, or a place in the cosmos. The Pascalian view is that the natural furnishings of reason and experience alone cannot do this. Nor can they establish for you whether or not there is a God. Whether you find your own life to be colossal or miniscule is determined by your heart and its connection to the universe. In the absence of God, though, what does this mean? I don't think we can definitively say that a nonreligious Pascalian view takes a stand on this. But even prior to exploring some options, it is evident that the general outline of Pascal's "cordate" epistemology can be fruitfully explored in a secular context. The question is how much further than this Pascal's thoughts can be secularized.

---

[1] Damasio, Antonio R. (1994). *Descartes' Error: Emotion, Reason, and the Human Brain.* New York: Putnam's Sons.

6 A Secular Pascalian Vision

6.1 Constraints on a Good Theory

The world, recall, is ambiguous to a Pascalian. This has both an epistemic and a metaphysical dimension.

Epistemically, on the subject's side of things, this means that depending on the state of your heart, you will see things in the world differently. The heart generates a will, to want or fear this or that. This then motivates one to look at one rather than another aspect of things, as we've discussed throughout the previous chapters. This amounts to what psychologists call "motivated reasoning," no matter what state your heart is in: all experience and all reasoning is motivated by some state of the heart. The way the world looks depends on your affective states.

Metaphysically, this means that the world is such that it can be interpreted in these different ways according to a subject's state of heart. This itself, for Pascal, is a significant fact about the world: it is ambiguous in nature. The world *could* have been totally clear-cut and unambiguous, appearing the same way no matter how a creature within it feels, or what aspect one looks at. Why does the world have available in it the properties that correspond to these different aspects? Why is the world perspectivally rich? Any worldview, even a secular one, should make sense of this.

There is something further to account for. A Pascalian view emphasizes the human condition as another feature in the world that needs to be accommodated. Philosophical theories should not float free, like abstract impressions, but rather remain true to actual human existence in the world. Pascal's description of our capacity for misery – the constant revolving desires, the pull of distractions, the self-obsession – seems as apt today as ever. But Pascal also holds that we can see, or feel, that we can be much better. We have some sort of conception of a much better life that we could be living. This should be accommodated by our metaphysical worldview as well.

Pascal's answer to the question of how to accommodate all these data was of course the Fall: this is how God made it so that some would see Him, and others would not, depending on what they want. We betrayed God and therefore by default are in a corrupted inner state. But in a secular version, we cannot appeal to the Fall. Indeed, Pascal's point was primarily that other *religions* cannot accommodate the ambiguity of the world (or the contrasting possible states of the subject); it isn't obvious what he would say about a sophisticated sort of naturalism of the sort only we today could formulate, with more recent insights from evolutionary theory, cognitive science, and physics. So the question for us is which worldviews can accommodate the ambiguity of the world manifested by the myriad ways we can perceive it and our inner struggles.

As a methodological point, then, any secular Pascalian vision will take the need to accommodate the foregoing data as a major factor in selecting theories. And we have seen that a Pascalian view is never a relativist one: there is one right answer. Furthermore, however we understand reality and our place in it, the heart has to play an explanatory part in how we can get things right (if we can get it right at all). That is, what is it about reality that the heart, if it can love what is objectively worthy of love, sets our reason and experience to work in a productive way, and what explains this possibility? This doesn't yet offer a Pascalian vision, but it does determine a Pascalian methodology for philosophy and puts substantial constraints on it.

6.2 The Good Prevails: James' Belief

In some of his work, much of which seems to me to have had Pascalian elements, William James came up with a rather broad notion of a "religious belief":

> ... religion says essentially two things.
> First, she says that the best things are the more eternal things, the overlapping things, the things in the universe that throw the last stone, so to speak, and say the final word ...
> The second affirmation of religion is that we are better off even now if we believe her first affirmation to be true. (*The Will to Believe*, X)

One way to interpret the first component is that the "best things" are the *morally* good things, that goodness will ultimately prevail. And the second component is that it is better for one to believe this, presumably because one then becomes happier and – as he suggests elsewhere – more useful to the world. That is, one is more useful for producing goodness, or helping it to become true that the good will prevail in the end. There is much to say about this idea, but here the point is that we can adopt such a view within a secular perspective, because it makes no mention of God, and certainly it does not depend on the Fall. This metaphysical worldview, which we can call 'James' belief', does not posit anything metaphysically exotic beyond moral goodness. Let us consider, then, what happens when we replace, *a la* James, God with Goodness, and posit that ultimately goodness will prevail over the absence of good. Does Pascal's view work with James' belief in place of the Fall?

The heart determines what aspects we see in the world. A heart that loves goodness – the good in the world, and its tendency (as one might believe it to be) to ultimately prevail – will see things and their significance differently than a heart that does not. Can you know the world better if you love goodness? According to James' belief, whatever course the history of the universe is on, it will end up favoring the good. So, loving goodness means, essentially, rooting for the right team, the winning team. Ultimately, the world will be as you want it to be, because things will work out for the good (in the end). Why does the world appear so awful to some people? The victory of the good things is still in progress; we are not at the end of history. Some parts of the world still are quite bad. This explains the ambiguity in the world with respect to James' belief. If we love the good, we should try to improve the things that are still bad – and again, ultimately, our side will win! The same kind of answer can be given if one asks why so many are prone to such internal misery, why they seek distractions, and so on: because they don't yet love the good, and the good will ultimately triumph. We are, without love of the good, losers.

This bare sketch shows that much of the structure of Pascal's view can be made to fit with a secular alternative. One might even replace goodness with something else, like nature or beauty.

Recall that what is needed in order to determine one's significance is an external anchor. And of course it is important to choose the right anchor. This is a genuine problem for James' view. How do you know, exactly, what the good things are that will prevail according to James' view? Moreover, it is a condition on this being a secular view that we can make sense of morality without God. Most philosophers today believe that to be the case, but the current view – Pascalianism with James' belief replacing the Fall – must be made to be compatible with such conceptions of secular goodness. So there is more work to do in developing this secular, Jamesian–Pascalian vision.

At any rate, you have no way to know by reason and experience whether James' view is true – that seems right, how could you know how history will end? This again is analogous to the Fall in Pascal, which is consistent with but not knowable by reason and experience operating on their own. So let us now consider a wager about James' belief.

6.3 Secular Wagers

In this concluding section, we will consider a wager, an argument for trying to change so that you become convinced, and are the kind of person who is drawn to James' belief. We can then compare some differences and similarities with Pascal's wager for God. Before considering James' belief in particular, it will help to get an idea of what a secular wager in general could look like. So let us consider a different secular wager first.

We have an enjoyable illustration in the 1969 Eric Rohmer film, *Ma Nuit Chez Maud* (My Night at Maud's), in which the characters discuss several of Pascal's ideas. In one scene, two friends discuss Pascal's wager. One of them, a Marxist, approvingly describes Pascal's wager applied to whether history has meaning – presumably, he means roughly that it matters how events in history unfold over time, and that in the long term eventually these historical events will culminate in a particular, inevitable, positive (Marxist) state. Perhaps he means, instead, simply that there is a teleological direction to human history, which tends toward a more and ultimately perfectly just situation. There are two hypotheses, he says: either history has meaning or it doesn't. He isn't sure which is right, in fact perhaps it is more likely that history has no meaning; there's a 90 percent chance it has no meaning, and a 10 percent chance it does. If he bets that it has no meaning, but it *does* have meaning, his whole life will be wasted, as he lives as if historical events don't matter, or have no ultimate direction or culmination. His life in that case is a wasted opportunity, one long and disappointing missing out on being part of history's trajectory and making a difference to what matters. Presumably this is because in such a life one is not politically engaged in the forces that shape history. So he must live according to the second hypothesis, that history has meaning, even if there's only a small chance that it is true. If he wins the bet, he will have lived as good and meaningful a life as he can, having believed truly, the whole time, that history has meaning, and having participated in and contributed (in however small a way) to the meaning and direction of historical events. On the other hand, if history has no meaning, then how could it matter that much what he spends his life doing? So there is not much to lose, in terms of meaning in life.

Fascinating as this dialogue is, notice that it ignores many of the complexities and nuances of Pascal's actual wager as described in the previous chapter. There is no distinction between forming a belief and getting into a state in which you can appreciate evidence that makes the belief reasonable. There is nothing about the advantages of believing that history has meaning even when in fact it doesn't. It will help to consider a different example to try to fill these gaps in the analogy.

Anyone who has tried to convey to a skeptical person excitement for a philosophical idea, a piece of music or art, or some other non-tangible item of significance will be familiar with the immovable grouch. You get into a song, say, and try to play it for your friend, excitedly watching their face for any hint of acknowledgment. You want to share the joy, and it would also be great to see the significance of the song confirmed by having someone else acknowledge it. But they are looking at their watch, their phone, the room ... they're bored and distracted. They could say, "whatever, it's just a bunch of notes." And are they wrong? Not technically: it is a bunch of notes. But you can describe *anything* like that. Instead, you might tell them about some philosophical idea about the world, how freedom seems incompatible with determinism, for example. But if they just don't feel the pull of the argument, or they just aren't interested in taking on the perspective from which this is important, they will again be bored: what's that got to do with what we're having for lunch? Some people cannot be moved, they are entirely earth-bound, stuck in the physical order of things. Their hearts are hardened to what you're trying to get them to acknowledge. This is not because they're incapable of understanding what you understand, at least not always. It is because they simply, as we say today, aren't feeling it – are not motivated to think about it long enough or as you do – in a charitable enough way to get it. This is a matter of the heart. Maybe, if they just *tried* to get into it, loosened up, the idea or the song would be compelling enough to move their heart. Or maybe not. They'll never know if they never try.

Perhaps it is you who are wrong, overly excited about this idea or song. Maybe it's right to wave it off without consideration. We can make some Pascalian observations here to understand and possibly challenge this impasse. Is the song important? Is your philosophical idea significant for our understanding of things? Presumably this depends on the world, and whether we think the world is that way is a function of our heart. So we lack any independent, God's-eye view of the matter. But notice that only one of you two has given the idea or song a chance, and that is you. You *know* that a human heart is capable of digging this song, for example, because you can dig it. Your friend doesn't *know* this because they haven't tried; they're closed off to the possibility.[2] Only you know *how* to dig it, even if you cannot convey that know-how to your friend. If there is much joy to be had by digging this song (and there usually is), and not much cost to trying to dig it, why not try to dig it? There is much joy to gain and little to lose. To refuse, to rest content with a hardened heart, seems unreasonable in at least this practical sense, all else equal (of course, if there are far better things to do with your time, that might make a difference to what it is reasonable to do). You should at least *try* not to have a hardened heart when there is something to gain from it and not much to lose, potentially. So, in this kind of scenario, one could argue that both sides are not equally reasonable merely because both are just going with their heart. One state of heart is preferable. That's the heart of one who digs the song or at least is open enough to try to.

---

[2] Herein lies a distinction between two different negative reactions to a song, and perhaps this generalizes to art and other things. One way to reject a song is to not get it, to never have experienced the aesthetic pull of the thing. This could be because you never tried, or tried and failed. It's possible that the song is just not lovable, but it's also possible that you simply don't get something that's there. The second way to reject a song is to have gotten it before, to understand the pull and appeal, but to reject that appeal. The song is "cheesy" we might say today, because you already get it, and are over it.

Now if your friend is reasonable and tries to dig it, but doesn't, we can conclude that the song isn't lovable enough or that your friend does not have an ear for music. Another possibility, mentioned before, is that you overreacted (positively) to the song. Or maybe circumstances weren't right for the truly great song to seduce your friend's ear, and some other time he *will* get it. Still, what did your friend lose? A few moments, maybe. But your friend did the reasonable thing and tried, and showed enough trust in you to give it this try. That's a good friend. At least, that's a better friend than the one who says: "No, I don't even want to hear it, I'm sure I won't like it and the fact that you do tells me nothing about whether it's any good." As if your friend doesn't trust that your experience and report of it was genuine or significant.

Suppose now instead that your friend *does* end up digging the song – I've written friends years after they recommended some music to me to tell them, "What was I thinking? You were right, this is amazing!" – do we say that your friend doesn't truly or honestly love it? Of course not. We say, at most, that what led to their loving it was your prodding. Kudos to you; good for your friend. Isn't friendship and an open heart great?

These analogies fit the Pascalian wager quite well, though there are still elements of Pascal's view that are absent. But having seen how close we can get in structure to Pascal's wager, we can now consider the same kind of reasoning applied to James' belief.

For Pascal, grasping at things for oneself ("concupiscence") is the source of our misery, in part because it obscures another, more worthwhile direction in which our heart pulls, namely God, the creator of those things. So, even though getting what you want might feel fun because desires are satisfied and itches are scratched, no *ultimate* satisfaction can result. We can understand this as an insight into the human condition even if we take goodness to be that external thing which we must love more than ourselves. It is a good psychological question whether those devoted to loving goodness (however that may manifest in their circumstances, taking care of vulnerable family members or others, working for a good cause) are healthier, less distracted, and feel less lost. I suspect so, but this isn't the place to analyze the evidence. It suffices to raise this as a possibility in order to see how it might play out in a secular Pascalian view.

6.3 Secular Wagers

Consider this speculation – I don't claim it is true, but it seems possible, and it would make the secular Pascalian view complete. When you love goodness, you see the world not only optimistically (at least, if you believe James' belief, that goodness will prevail) but you also see the world as mediating this goodness, so that events and things are parts of the process of the world becoming better. You need not think that awful tragedies are good, of course. But you can understand this as part of the process of the eventual triumph of goodness. Perhaps, then, when you love the good, you are inclined to accept James' belief. And in order to reap the benefits of believing in James' belief, including leading a charmed life knowing, and feeling, that you are contributing to the triumph of goodness, it helps if you *love* goodness. Otherwise, what's so great about helping goodness to prevail?

It may turn out that James' belief is false. But if you believe it, you still lived a charmed life, one in which you did your best to do what conforms to the good as you understood and loved it and were quite possibly happier for so acting. This is not such a bad thing to risk. If it turns out that James' belief is true, then your life will have been part of the process of the triumph of good over evil, or at least it will have been an attempt. This may not be the infinite reward of Pascal's theology, but it is, we might say, a maximal reward in terms of your life's purpose. You lived a good life, and how much better does it get in a secular framework?

Now we can see that wagering on James' belief, in the sense of seeking a heart that is conducive to it, is clearly the best move. Maybe it is true, maybe not. It is better for you to wager that it is, because you risk only a pleasant life at worst, and at best your life has maximal purpose and you contribute to that which you love, goodness. You even help, in your own small way, to bring about the *truth* of James' belief by pursuing goodness as a lover of goodness. This seems a reasonable wager. But how do you come to *love* goodness? You can try by emulating those who do. But whether you ultimately come to love goodness depends not only on your efforts but also on whether goodness is lovable, whether you are so constituted as to be capable of loving and seeing the world in that way, and whether the world around actually *does* manifest goodness in a way that makes James' belief true. It would be better, and an instance of goodness' triumph, if you loved it.

Suggested Further Reading

The following are recommended books for further reading as both background and explorations of the themes discussed in this book.

On Pascal in General

Ariew, Roger & Avnur, Yuval (2025). *A Companion to Pascal*. Hoboken, New Jersey: Wiley.

Kołakowski, Leszek (1995). *God Owes Us Nothing: A Brief Remark on Pascal's Religion and on the Spirit of Jansenism*. Chicago: University of Chicago Press.

Moriarty, Michael (2020). *Pascal: Reasoning and Belief*. New York: Oxford University Press.

On Pascal's Epistemology

Cottingham, John (ed.) (1996). *Descartes: Meditations on First Philosophy: With Selections from the Objections and Replies*. New York: Cambridge University Press.

Garber, Daniel (2009). *What Happens after Pascal's Wager: Living Faith and Rational Belief*. Milwaukee: Marquette University Press.

James, William (1995). *The Will to Believe: And Other Writings from William James*. New York: Image Books. Edited by Trace Murphy.

Montaigne, Michel de (2003). *Apology for Raymond Sebond*. Indianapolis: Hackett.

Penelhum, Terence (1983). God and Skepticism. *Philosophical Studies Series*, no. 28 Dordrecht: D. Reidel Publishing.

On Pascal's Religious Outlook

Clark, Gillian (ed.) (1995). *Augustine: Confessions Books I–Iv*. New York: Cambridge University Press.

Schellenberg, John (1993). *Divine Hiddenness and Human Reason*. Ithaca: Cornell University Press.

Wettstein, Howard (2012). *The Significance of Religious Experience*. New York: Oxford University Press USA.

Index

Abraham, 39, 57, 60, 130
Adam and Eve, 63
affect, 2, 36, 50, 71, 75, 78, 110, 133, 134
agnosticism, 78–83, 115, 120
al-Ghazali, Abu Hamid, 24
Alter, Robert, 20
ambiguity, 3, 11, 57, 59, 65, 68, 72–90, 123, 125, 134, 135
Anselm, 82
apologetics, 5, 15, 37, 91, 107, 109, 123
artificial intelligence (AI), 33, 35
atheism, 39, 78, 79, 80, 81, 82, 93, 115, 121, 130
Augustine, 2, 8, 10, 20, 43, 47, 56, 59, 60, 65, 69, 91, 112, 113, 132

beatitude, 115, 118
Becker, Ernest, 99
Bible, 30, 39, 47, 56, 57, 60, 78, 91, 92, 129, 130
  Book of Ecclesiastes, 30, 92, 94, 98, 102, 104
  Book of Exodus, 47
  Book of Isaiah, 20, 42, 47, 48, 56
  Book of Psalms, 47, 57, 67, 114
  Book of Romans, 48
  Song of Songs, 129
Borges, Jorge Luis, 29
Buber, Martin, 41, 67
Buddhism, 100

calculator, invention of, 4, 35
Calvin, John, 38
Camus, Albert, 34
Charron, Pierre, 15
Christianity, 2–5, 9, 13–16, 37, 39, 43, 48, 57, 59, 61, 65, 72–75, 104, 105, 109, 114, 116, 123, 132
Chuang-Zi, 33
Cicero, 38

concupiscence, 11, 61, 63, 65, 93, 94, 98, 103, 110, 111, 120–123, 140
conspiracy theories, 3, 85–90
conversion, 109

Damásio, António R., 133
David, 57, 67, 68, 78, 112, 114
Davidson, Donald, 109
de Roannes, Mlle, 20
Deism, 39, 60, 74, 75, 105, 123
Descartes, René, 1–12, 24, 54, 55, 60, 132, 133
desire, 18, 19, 48, 50, 51, 91–105, 110, 127
  wrongness of, 96
diversion, 99–103
Divine hiddenness, 42, 55–60, 65, 68, 70, 73, 74, 75, 85, 104, 114, 130
dreams, 22–26
Dylan, Bob, 49

echo chambers, 86, 87
Eliot, T.S., 1
epistemology, 10, 64, 68, 70, 71, 87, 88, 113, 117, 124, 127, 133, 134
Euclid, 18, 53

faith, 58
fine-tuning argument, 77
following the believers, 120, 121, 141
Frankfurt, Harry, 61

Garber, Daniel, 125
garden of Eden, 93
geometry, 13, 15, 16, 17, 20, 28, 29, 45, 49, 52, 53, 71, 124, 132
God
  angry, 59
  God of the philosophers, 59, 60, 74, 75, 78

Index

help from, 63
knowing, 112
personal God, 60, 77
proofs of God's existence. *See* proofs of God's existence
Gödel, Kurt, 33, 34
goodness, 135–136, 140, 141
Grace, 2, 43, 61, 65, 94, 109, 113, 127, 129, 130, 131
heart, 13, 20–21, 46–71, 80–83, 88, 89–90, 133–136
centrality of, 1–12
change of, 2, 12, 63, 93, 94, 98, 99, 104–105, 109–112, 121, 123, 125, 127, 130
cultivating love in, 76
intuition of, 39–40
pathology of, 94, 98
Hume, David, 6, 15, 25, 41, 54, 116
Huxley, T.H., 79, 83

infinity, 5, 12, 29, 35, 37, 106, 109, 111, 118, 122, 125
Isaac, 130

James, William, 41, 82, 93, 116, 117, 136, 137, 140, 141
Jansen, Cornelius, 8, 113, 132
Jesus Christ, 15, 61
justice, 60, 64, 113, 131

Kahneman, Daniel, 27
Kant, Immanuel, 2, 35, 53
Kierkegaard, Søren, 94
Kolakowsi, Lezek, 43
Kunda, Ziva, 18

Leibniz, Gottfried Wilhelm, 132
love of God, 61, 68, 70, 73, 83, 98

Malcolm, Norman, 59
Marxism, 137
misery, 91, 93, 96, 98, 99, 102, 105, 108, 125, 134, 136, 140
misinformation, 85
Montaigne, Michel de, 8, 10, 15, 38, 44
Moore, G.E., 17, 41, 42
Moriarty, Michael, 8, 32, 53, 92
mortality, 92, 93, 98, 99, 112

Moses, 56, 57
motivated reasoning, 18, 19, 49, 50, 51, 88, 134

Nagel, Thomas, 31

paganism, 56, 75, 123
pantheism, 56
Pascal's works
"The Memorial", 56
A Conversation with M. Sacy, 44
Pensées, 5, 6, 92
The Art of Persuasion, 15, 16, 18, 19, 84, 121
The Geometrical Mind, 15, 16, 17, 29, 48
Three Discourses on the Condition of the Great, 30
Pascalianism, 137
permissivism, 11
perspectivism, 83, 87, 134
Pharoah, 47, 52, 53, 55
Plantinga, Alvin, 70, 77
Popkin, Richard, 15
pornography, 102
Port Royal (convent), 5
probability theory, 4
proofs of God's existence, 3, 21, 38–45, 54, 66, 68, 69, 72, 73, 76–78, 80, 82, 113, 119, 132
public transit, 4

relativism, 73, 79, 80, 90, 135
religion as rational, 83
religious experience, 70–71
Rohmer, Eric, 137

Sacks, Rabbi Jonathan, 47
salvation, 14, 39, 40, 63, 82, 110, 113, 121
Schellenberg, John, 42, 130
Schopenhauer, Arthur, 94
secularism, 85, 95, 98, 105, 134–137, 140
seeking God, 43, 62, 81, 82, 119–122
self-interest, 52, 111, 112, 115, 121, 123, 124, 128
self-love, 95–98, 102, 111, 112
Sellier, Philippe, 9, 92
skepticism, 1–12, 25–45, 52, 54, 132, 133
insufficiency of reason and experience, 1–12, 17, 19, 25–28, 32–36, 39, 40, 49, 63, 64, 82, 87, 98, 103, 115, 124, 132, 133, 137

Smith, Adam, 6
social media, 88, 92, 97, 100, 102
Solomon, 92, 94, 98, 102, 104
Spinoza, Baruch, 61, 132

Teresa of Avila, 71
The Fall, 11, 21, 37, 43, 44, 56, 59–65, 71, 75, 78, 83, 85, 93, 98, 103–105, 114, 119, 123, 125, 129, 132, 134–137
theism, 75, 78, 82, 84
thinking well, 100, 103, 105
truth, 89, 90, 96, 99, 101, 106, 109–110, 115, 116–117, 119

loving, 85, 90
rejection of, 97

unhappiness, 99–103

vacuum, existence of, 4
vanity, 50, 51, 94, 96, 97, *See* self-love
Voltaire, 6

wager, 4–6, 12, 82, 106–131
 secular wager, 137–141
 source of, 4
 standard description of, 107
Wittgenstein, Ludwig, 6

For EU product safety concerns, contact us at Calle de José Abascal, 56–1°,
28003 Madrid, Spain or eugpsr@cambridge.org.

www.ingramcontent.com/pod-product-compliance
Lightning Source LLC
LaVergne TN
LVHW011835060526
838200LV00053B/4046